"SHUT THOSE THICK LIPS!"
·A Study of Slum School Failure

GERRY ROSENFELD

State University of New York at Buffalo

Waveland Press, Inc.

Prospect Heights, Illinois

For information about this book, write or call:

Waveland Press, Inc.
P.O. Box 400
Prospect Heights, Illinois 60070
(312) 634-0081

Foreword

About the Author

Gerry Rosenfeld was born in New York City, the son of immigrant parents. His schooling took place in that city and he later taught in a Harlem elementary school for five and a half years. It was that experience which afforded him the material for this book, while he was completing his doctorate in anthropology and education at Columbia University Teachers College. At present he is professor of anthropology at the State University of New York at Buffalo. His primary interests are in applied and urban anthropology, and anthropology and education. He is a Fellow of the American Anthropological Association and the Society for Applied Anthropology.

About the Book

This is a "passionate ethnography" of a single school, but it is more than a case study of that school. It is an analysis, normative in character but based upon fact, of the conditions of slum schooling in the United States of America. What it means to go to a slum school and to be a black child becomes abundantly clear. It becomes clear also why the achievement of minority children in school is low. As a participant-observer the author was able to combine the behavioral and anecdotal record in Harlem School with a social scientific assessment of its import.

The teachers and the children in this environment interact in a deadly cycle of self-sustaining perceptions. Teachers see children as uneducable. Children see teachers as hostile, the school as forbidding, the experience as limiting and destructive. The children themselves reflect an environment that is a bleeding ulcer on the face of the "richest nation in the world." The teachers reflect other environments—less desperate but inadequate as preparation for life.

But people are not passive. The children "act out": they strike back both at the teacher and the school and at themselves.

The author shows how, as a teacher in the very school he describes, he captured some of the energy produced out of frustration and in so doing demonstrated potentials for learning that are usually assumed to be absent among children of the poor, and, given the conditions of both school and community, might very well be presumed to have been lost. An important conclusion which Professor Rosenfeld draws from his study is that the teacher focuses on the child as being different and disadvantaged rather than upon the

iii

interactional setting in which cultural transmission is taking place.

It is in the demonstration of capabilities in the children and in the educative act that the hope lies for change. And change there must be if the American dream is not to turn out as a mawkish nightmare.

George and Louise Spindler

Why *"Shut Those Thick Lips!"*

Most persons have become familiar with the overt hostility directed toward black children in so many public school classrooms. Less apparent, but even more profound, is the covert prejudice of some teachers against these same children. The subtle character of this kind of behavior does not diminish its negative impact, nor can we "explain away" this behavior because it was "unintended." Anthropology has continually sought to probe the unprobed, to seek meaning in acts beyond their manifestation. It is for this reason that the quote "Shut those thick lips!" is used as the title for this book about a Harlem school. Perhaps the teacher who repeatedly used this phrase was unaware of its portent. Even more reason then to explicate the character of life which children are forced to endure in the slum school. By descriptively revealing this reality we can hope to make the necessary revisions in the schools. *"Shut Those Thick Lips!"* is not intended to inflame. That is relatively easy to accomplish. It is, rather, intended to inform. How one thereafter uses information is a matter the reader may resolve.

Acknowledgments

Many persons have contributed, knowingly and otherwise, to my thinking about the education of children from the point of view of anthropology. Gratitude is owed each of them. It was John Collier who, while I was an undergraduate, first infused me with the spirit of anthropology, and who, by his own example, represented for all who were his students the most humane tradition in anthropological inquiry. Conrad Arensberg, too, by his teaching and encouragement helped me to understand the meaning of community and the relationship of the school to the community of which it is a part. His writings on community study and the approach of the applied anthropologist are rendered with clarity and relevance.

Lambros Comitas was most helpful when help was most needed. His advice on methodology and the ordering of data was instrumental in making clear to me the need for organizing fragments of information into substantive evidence. Otherwise my writing might have been little more than a personal essay. And to Solon Kimball goes my appreciation for what he has taught me and the opportunity to work in personal association with him as my study proceeded through its initial stages. His influence can hardly be measured. Most of what I know in anthropology was learned from him. His thoughts and ideas are interspersed in many ways on these pages, and I hope he is faithfully represented.

Alexander Lesser and Lazer Goldberg, as close friends and colleagues, continually forced me to extend my thinking beyond normal limitations and I owe many personal insights to their constant probing and personal influence. Each is a man whose perceptions broadened and fused with my own. Murray Bergson, Porter Kirkwood, George McLain, and John van Buren are others with whom I shared various ideas. They all deserve credit.

Finally, and primarily, my thanks go to the children of Harlem whom I came to teach but learned to learn from. They were the first and lasting influence in this writing. Each of their names should be cited capitally here. I hope they would regard my portrayal of them as accurate and fair. The imprint they made on my life far outweighs the impact I may have made on theirs. And I am wholly confident that the teaching they will give their own children will far surpass the teaching I gave them. The children of Harlem have long persevered, and it cannot be too distant in the future when their endurance will have given rise to better educational procedure for themselves and all other children.

G. L. R.

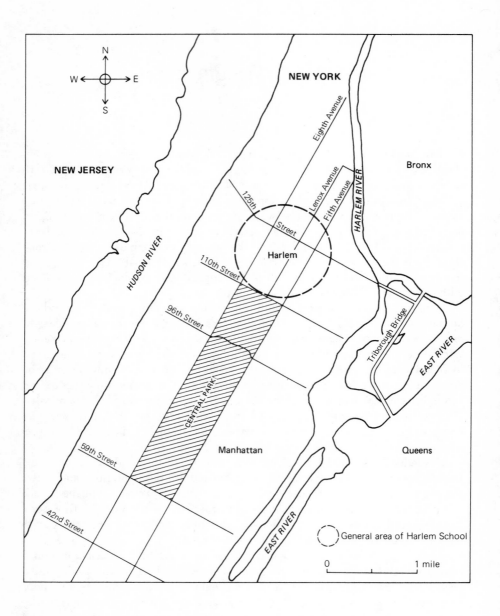

Contents

1 / Introduction

IT IS DIFFICULT to contemplate what our culture would be like had we no
schools. It may, in fact, be an open question as to whether we would be
better off as a people or not. To the same extent it is equally hard to know
what definitive impact schooling has on the lives of particular children. We do
know this, however: not all children benefit equally from schooling; not all
children like school. Indeed, for children of the urban poor, school is down-
right oppressive. For the black child in Harlem it serves as a symbol of the
larger society's racism and callous disregard for those it intends to exclude
socially. It is not surprising then that the schools occupy a prominent place in
our thinking. "Community control," "dissent," "relevance," and "change" are
all terms familiarly associated with schooling. What follows in these pages is an
attempt to lend meaning to these concerns, borne of personal experience in a
Harlem elementary school for more than five years.

What perhaps characterizes this description as a partial departure from other
works is its attempt to combine the behavioral and anecdotal record with a
social scientific assessment of its import. This, therefore, is a cultural study of
a slum school, told from the vantage point of one who was a teacher there.
It is not a traditional anthropological study in that it cannot be termed an
ethnographic study in the strict sense. At best it is a partial ethnography. I
shared in the lives of children at school, but not in the totality of their lives.
Much is intuitive and personal, somewhat of a phenomenological appraisal of
events. No attempt to hide a point of view is made. On the contrary, it is
hoped that an informed point of view emerges. One needs to take a stand on
issues when people's lives are involved, and the lives of children are what is at
stake in the slum school. Not to articulate ideological preferences in such
instances seems to me to strip such studies of their justification. Anthropology,
I think, has begun to evolve toward a period when the participant-observer
does more than share events in the lives of people; he shares their concerns
as well. He may even find justification in pleading and supporting causes they
recognize.

The teacher of children is very much like a participant-observer (P. Bohannan 1968:161–166). He himself may be informant, friend, confidant, or
"outsider" to his children in class. Hence, many of the problems and concerns
of the field researcher are found in the teaching situation. Pitfalls and rewards

1

lie along the way, each following from the teacher's own behavior. As he comes to regard children as the "host" or "recipient" culture, he begins to see himself as a change agent, often having to make immediate judgments that have impact on his relationship with them and on their well-being. He thus must gain insight into the classroom as a culture system and learn to view the school as a social system, just as classroom and school together need to be juxtaposed with the larger society of which they are a part. Most of us are agreed that the school very often represents, in microcosm, the larger macrocosm—the culture. By looking at one slum school we may be assisted in understanding other schools and perhaps thereby gain insight into the enculturation process: the means by which each person assumes a relationship to his culture.

A basic assumption in this writing is that one can report honestly and responsibly on events that affected him personally. Moreover, it suggests that one has an obligation to describe faithfully what is, to him, indefensible and morally corrupt treatment of children by some educators in schools. It is hoped in this way that social science is served, not undermined.

> Perhaps our greatest responsibility is as teachers. We must show . . . by our example that . . . honesty, not neutrality, is the prerequisite for good teaching and for good scholarship; that knowledge legitimately leads to informed opinion as well as fact; to understanding of consequences as well as causes; to commitment to act as well as to consider. We must show . . . that humanity is not incompatible with science; that science without humanity is indeed a monster and that social science without humanity is a contradiction in terms as well; that we are proud to join . . . in placing ourselves squarely on the side of mankind, unashamed to wish mankind well, and that we will not sell our souls for money or professional advantage to the anti-human forces in society (Berreman 1968: 855).

I also believe that the reader ought to share with the writer the burden of clarifying issues of social import. I state the case as I see it. Others may react and restate things as they choose. "Every cobbler thinks leather is the only thing. Most social scientists . . . have their favorite research methods with which they are familiar and have some skill in using. And I suspect we mostly choose to investigate problems that seem vulnerable to attack through these methods. But we should at least try to be less parochial than cobblers" (Trow 1957:35).

Schools are, at the least, interesting institutions for study. They have a remarkable resiliency, sometimes seemingly impervious to promptings to change them. We are all products of the schools. Each of us has internalized in major ways their impact on us. Particularly in the slum, however, schools often function to reduce children to a common denominator, serving to disenchant and alienate them. Continued efforts at in-school ethnography are needed to better understand this process and to clarify the private and spontaneous aspects of school life, as well as their "common sense" public images. It seems to me, for example, that much of what happens in the Harlem school is played out in a context of institutional and personal crisis. Is it normal for children and teachers to see their existence together as a crisis? Who in this situation should really be the focus for study? The child? The teacher? The "system"? What, in fact, makes for a "bad" school?

The culture concept has too often been absent in seeking answers to these questions. This study tries very hard to incorporate that absent perspective. Children have told us by their behavior that our conceptions of them are false. New images are needed, for it is quite clear that our schools are often very, very bad.

2 / "Sixty-six sixty-sevenths": becoming a teacher

SCHOOLING IN AMERICA is the primary means by which children are to acquire the knowledge necessary for fullest participation in our culture. To accomplish this with the least margin for error, it is mandated that children attend school beginning at age five or six. Throughout the nation, children at this age are made to embark on an extended rite of passage[1] which will carry them into young adulthood. So convinced are we of the necessity of this prolonged ritual for the child that virtually no formal alternatives to schooling exist. Even the children, who have no say about whose hands will guide their schooling, seemingly accede to its requirements. Should there be a person born in this country who did not go to school, he would appear strange indeed, somehow having escaped a major experience in growing up.

Despite this universal aspect of schooling in our country, it is clear that education in our schools does not have the same impact on all children. Some are receptive to the school's promptings, while others are resistive. The causes for differentials in attainment and response in school may be sought in a number of places. Certainly not all children react in the same way even to the same stimulus; not all children are initially made to interpret the meaning of public schooling in the same way; and communities, almost all of which contain schools, are not to be seen as identical, historically or culturally. The teacher too is a factor. Neither teachers nor school officials perceive the teaching task and the children uniformly. Even were children presumed "genetically equal," the differences in their prior experiences and the differences in teachers' perceptions would eventually create differences in academic results.

The recruitment of children for a public school education is more standard than the product which is the result of this education. The recruitment of teachers, the conveyers of the culture, is less consistent. Though most persons are prepared for teaching in formal teacher preparation programs, some come to public education through the "back door." My own experience was of such a kind. I was only minimally prepared, if at all, to teach children, but was allowed to attain the formal credentials once already on the job.

---

[1] See van Gennep (1960). The author discusses in cross-cultural perspective the meaning and importance of rites of passage in people's lives and how they assume new status positions in their cultures.

I came to Harlem at the start having become a teacher largely by chance. At the time I was a graduate student in anthropology at a local university. Seeking work to supplement the income needed to support a growing family, I was advised by a friend to become an elementary schoolteacher. I thought this suggestion to be absurd because I had no qualifications for being a schoolteacher either by prior experience or formal education. However, my friend informed me that anyone with an earned college degree, even in a field other than education, was eligible to apply for examination as Substitute Teacher of Common Branch Subjects in New York City. I assured my friend that I would not pass the examination in any case. He, in turn, convinced me that he had become a teacher in just this manner. "If I passed the test," he said, "you'll pass it too." I soon came to believe him.

I also learned that one would be given three years after passing the examination to achieve thirty-six college credits in education to validate his teaching license. One could, however, find employment as a teacher during this time, with two years of full-time teaching counting as twelve credits toward the thirty-six point requirement. Further, even as a substitute teacher one could seek full-time employment in a school. One might have substitute teacher status, but be hired by a school as a regular teacher assigned to his own class. More than this, being a substitute teacher had some particular advantages. A person was not assigned to a school by the Board of Education, but could seek his own employment at schools of his choice. If the teacher was hired by a school, the Board of Education approved and verified the placement. Starting salaries were the same for substitutes and regular teachers. It all sounded much easier than I had previously assumed. The teaching profession was hardly a "closed" society, but rather open to people of diverse preparation and persuasion.

My original objectives in wanting to teach were simple. The Harlem community seemed the ideal location for these preferences. I wanted employment near the university where I was studying; I wanted to teach children for whom public schooling had not always been a profitable and happy experience, hoping that I could learn to teach well and be of service to them. I also had the latent notion in mind that teaching experience in Harlem might someday provide me with interesting descriptive material for anthropological study. Though these priorities were altered and rearranged somewhat once I began teaching, they were the initial spurs to my teaching anticipations.

I made application for the examination for substitute teacher and was later summoned with other applicants to take the written part of the test.[2] It was given over two days and consisted of an essay part and short answers to questions of general academic knowledge. My lack of formal preparation in education courses did not prove a handicap to me. The essay part of the examination entailed a brief discussion of "vandalism" and was judged pri-

---

[2] The examination was given March 11–12, 1957. An oral part of the examination was given on May 28, 1957. The combination score of these two parts decided the applicant's eligibility for licensing as a substitute teacher.

marily for language usage, not content. I felt confident of my performance.

Two months later I received notification to appear for the oral part of the examination. When I arrived for this test, I was surprised by its brevity and substance. At first I was cautioned by the examiner to speak in a "moderate" voice while he sat at the rear of the room. I was made to say "Long Island," "singing," and "sixty-six sixty-sevenths." I was instructed to repeat these several times and was then asked if sibilant sounds had always given me difficulty. Though I had not found this a prior concern, I thought it best to volunteer that I would work hard to make this aspect of my speech pattern more acceptable. I was given remedial lessons for a minute or two by the examiner and then cordially dismissed. The entire examination lasted no more than fifteen minutes.

Friends, thereafter, told me that I must have passed the examination, for it was customary practice to send those who initially failed to one or two additional examiners. Two months later their confidence was supported. I was informed by the Board of Examiners that my substitute teacher credentials would be forthcoming.[3]

"YOU CAN START AT THE BOTTOM"

I wasted little time. I had been told of an elementary school in Harlem that was in need of teachers for the next school year. I arranged an appointment with the principal within the week[4] and headed for Harlem School.[5]

I was very courteously received by the principal, Mr. Hecht. He described the nature of the teaching task at Harlem School and informed me there was a position open for a "regular substitute"; that is, I could be assigned as the regular teacher of my own class, even though I held a substitute teacher's certificate. I would have the same responsibilities as any other full-time teacher.

During my interview Mr. Green, the assistant principal for grades five and six, joined us. He too made me feel at ease and explained that the children at Harlem School posed significant problems for teachers. Most of the children were described as from economically poor homes who had to make do without the niceties that wealthier children enjoy. Often, I was told, the children represented learning and discipline problems for teachers and that a "strong hand" had to be taken with them. He also submitted that on occasion children do well in school despite the fact that most of them were two or more years behind expected levels of achievement by the time they reached sixth grade.

This was all rather new to me and I was not at that time certain of the real implications of this information. Moreover, I wondered about my ability to

---

[3] This notification arrived on June 15, 1957. I was now permitted to seek a job as a teacher.
[4] This took place on the morning of June 20, 1957.
[5] "Harlem School" will hereafter be the words used to identify the school herein described. Similarly all names have been changed to preserve the identity and integrity of persons being described.

be of service to the children at Harlem School. Mr. Green continued the interview and asked other questions of me: Had I worked with children before? How many college credits had I earned in education? Did I intend to make teaching a career?

I had anticipated the questions and answered them as honestly as I could, which brought smiles of sympathy and understanding from the faces of Mr. Hecht and Mr. Green.

"Are you in good health? You look strong enough," said Mr. Green.

"You aren't hiring me for my health, are you?"

"No. But we can always use men in a school like this."

It was apparent that my maleness stood me in good stead. Most elementary schoolteachers are women, and men who show any potential promise as teachers are welcomed to Harlem School. If, indeed, the disciplining of children is a major concern, men were seen as temperamentally relevant to the task. This seemed to be their point of view.

Finally, Mr. Hecht asked: "Are you sure you have no experience?"

"I'm sure," I said.

"Good," said Mr. Green. "You can start at the bottom and work yourself up. Give him an 'Opportunity Class,' Mr. Hecht."

When I asked what an "Opportunity Class" was, I was told it was a class made up of children who underachieved in school and who sometimes posed an array of "emotional" and learning problems. I was told not to worry about it, however; if I could do any kind of job with them, my efforts would be appreciated.

When I left Harlem School that day, having been hired as a teacher, I reflected on the school and my interview. It had been very informal. The school was very old. The principal and the assistant principal seemed personable and friendly. It was much easier than I thought it would be. Suddenly I realized—I had not even been asked my first name! Was it because I was being hired to fill a "slot" rather than for my personal qualifications? I wondered about this now.

3 / Opportunity class

DURING THE SUMMER I contemplated the approaching job. I conferred with friends who were teachers and tried to prepare myself for the task of teaching fifth-grade children. New teachers to Harlem School were to report for work two days before the opening of classes. On that day I was introduced to the other new teachers, school officials I had not met, the clerical staff, and various specialists in subject fields. I was then shown to my classroom. The remedial reading teacher met with us after that and told us there would be special help for the teachers of "Op" classes (the Opportunity Classes). We were told not to be surprised or discouraged by the low reading levels of the children. With encouragement they would improve. We were to estimate children's reading levels by giving informal reading tests, and then we would be given the appropriate books for them.

On the next day all regularly assigned teachers arrived, and rosters of classes and children's record cards were distributed. I would have seventeen children in my class, such a low number usually being reserved for "more difficult" classes. Average class size, I learned, was otherwise about thirty-five children. There were ten boys and seven girls in Op-5 (my class), which was the "last" class on the grade. All of the children were recorded as two or more years below grade level in reading. IQ's ranged from ninety to below seventy. I was not sure what this meant, so I searched the children's record cards for whatever additional information I could glean. Not only was there provision for noting the children's academic achievement, but a behavioral record was included as well. I wondered about some of the categories used for depicting children's behavior and how their previous teachers decided on the entries present. For example, in the category "Attitude toward group control" there were three subheadings from which to choose: "Usually nonconforming," "Occasionally resists group control," and "Responds well to group control." For almost every child the first choice had been marked. Was this good or bad? If a child is nonconforming, is he more creative than the conforming child? Is he more curious and mentally active? Or is he antagonistic and unresponsive?

As a new teacher I found it difficult to interpret the record card entries without knowing the children personally. Some categories were fairly clear, I supposed. Under "Work habits," for instance, the entry "Generally works with sustained attention" seemed to indicate past experience during which the child's interest had been engaged. However, even here it was not revealed in which subject matter the child showed this response. What puzzled me most was the last category on this balance sheet: "Relationship to parents." For most of the children the subcategory checked was "Parent-child relationship seems disturbed." How did teachers know this to be the case? Had they met all the parents? Was this an entry made automatically if a child was thought to be a discipline problem? Was school performance the result of the child's relationship to his parents? Or was such an entry on the record card more presumptuous than factual? My curiosity about the children and the school had been aroused even before classes had begun.

THE INITIATION PERIOD

The children at Harlem School find themselves there because they live in the neighborhood. The teachers, however, arrive from points both near and distant. They came from every borough of New York City and from New Jersey, Long Island, and Westchester and Rockland Counties. Several teachers had served at Harlem School for almost twenty years. Mr. Hecht and Mr. Green had many years of service in the school. I was clearly a beginner, and I felt like one.

When I arrived for the first day of classes, I suddenly felt conspicuous as I walked from the subway station. It seemed as if I were being watched. I knew this was not the case of course, but I still had the feeling that my personal thoughts were open to everyone I passed. Almost no white persons live in black Harlem and those white people who do appear during the day are those who work there: delivery men, policemen, store owners, and teachers. My style of dress and the books I carried doubtlessly revealed my identity as a teacher, and several persons smiled and nodded as I passed. This too left me uncertain, but I resolved to behave "normally," which was an indication perhaps of the difficulty I felt in doing so. I was not altogether unfamiliar with Harlem, having attended college in a section of Harlem and having spent many days at the Schomburg Library Collection not far away. Indeed, I thought to myself, as a younger person I had visited the Apollo Theatre with black friends; but, those friends not withstanding, my uncertainty and lack of full confidence about what loomed ahead in the classroom rendered me cautious and anticipating.[1]

After checking in at the school office, I went to meet my class in the inside yard. I reflected on the "forbidding facade" of Harlem School and how it seemed to blend in with the deteriorating tenements surrounding it. When I had approached from a distance, I could distinguish the school only by the American flag waving out front. At closer sight one could see the grate-covered windows which revealed the institutional character of the building: "a high,

---

[1] This is the mild and initial sense of "culture shock" that beginning teachers often express at Harlem School. It refers to the inability to understand events in another cultural setting by means of one's normally developed perceptive mechanisms. It sometimes results in the person's denigration of others who represent for him the "different" culture.

narrow, bleak structure like an Edwardian jail, where . . . kids from the most leprously rundown part of Harlem get their primary schooling."[2]

Inside, the school was well maintained, having been made ready for the new school year over the summer. The dimly lit structure was laid out in the form of two "y's" on each landing extending in opposite directions. On its five floors the vertical of the "y" contained an inside yard on the first floor, an auditorium on the second floor, and a gymnasium on the fifth floor. On the third and fourth floors, the vertical contained classrooms. The arms or wings of the "y" also contained classrooms. The school office was on the second floor, and the first floor also had a cafeteria and the nurse's office. Doors led in from the front of the school and out the back as well. In the hours between 9 A.M. and 3 P.M. almost 1,800 children and 75 teachers filtered into and out of the building.

When I met the children, they greeted me in friendly fashion and asked if I were a new teacher (they did not recognize me from their previous year's experience). They expressed the hope that I would be "nice." We climbed to our assigned room, room 515, amid first day excitement. When I opened the door, we found a pigeon flying about the room. "I'll get the mother-fucker," murmured a child in enthusiasm, and he grabbed for the window pole in the corner. As he swatted back and forth, I ran to open all the windows so the pigeon might escape. It was finally driven out, while the chain-hung lamps rocked from the window pole thrusts. Miraculously none of them had been broken. I soon realized that the pigeon had entered the room from outside through an open window that would not stay closed. This subsequently was to be a problem on cold winter days.

"Hey teach, can I be the window monitor?" asked the boy with the pole.

"Only when pigeons are in the room," I answered.

With this he sat down proudly, the pole still in hand. I assured him we could return the pole to the corner, and I stood there as giggles accompanied each child to his seat. Class was now in session!

We proceeded to make seating arrangements, and I then checked attendance. I saw nineteen children, but I had expected seventeen. We soon discovered that two children belonged elsewhere, having come to room 515 because that was their classroom the year before. I asked the children to write their names and addresses on sheets of paper so that I could gain an initial sense of how they wrote. I then mused through a pamphlet given to me when I had arrived that morning. It said:

> A pleasing voice can be developed by almost anyone who will give a little time and thought to its cultivation. The exercises necessary for the attainment of this attribute are simple, and they mean much to the teacher from the standpoint of health.
>
> Regard for throat and lung hygiene, as well as professional propriety, should make us avoid shrillness, and stridency of tone, which strain and injure the throat, and which indicate lack of breeding and ultimately destroy the teacher's influence on the class. . . .

---

[2] Alsop (1964:26). The phrase "forbidding facade" is used in this article to describe the outside appearance of Harlem School.

Remember, "The voice with the smile wins." The old adage, "if you bring a smiling visage to the glass, you meet a smile," is true. Change "glass" to "class," and you have the key to the situation (New York City Board of Education 1929:36–37).

This advice gave little to smile about; it offered little of practical insight. I soon discovered that most of the children were on a second-grade reading level and that some could barely read at all. One child, Rosa, had arrived only during the summer from Puerto Rico and knew virtually no English. She apparently was put into our class because there were no classes for non-English speaking children at Harlem School. It was not long before I learned that Opportunity Classes were really made up of children who were taken from other classes because hope had been abandoned by school officials that the children could learn. Presumably by removing them from other classes in the grades, those other classes would function better. In the teachers' cafeteria (really an unused classroom) I learned that the Opportunity Classes were the "dumping ground" for children the school discarded.

This surprised me for several reasons. The children themselves seemed alert and active; why couldn't they learn? And, if they were already so far behind in their work, why was I, an inexperienced teacher, assigned to them? Did they not require, and deserve, the best teachers in the school? I could find no immediate answers to these questions.

My first days on the job left me bewildered and with a sore throat, but with no teaching insights. It seemed that the variety of lessons I had prepared over the summer were either already used up or not fitting. The barrage of directives from the school office about attendance, fire drills, assembly periods, trips, and other school business left me further confused. I felt like a small, anonymous cog in a great big wheel that managed to keep running despite my difficulties. At first I wondered if I were the only one so inept, but I soon found that even teachers who had been at Harlem School for a number of years were expressing disgust and disappointment. Lunch period among the teachers was like a locker room session after a ballgame, with each teacher complaining about the children in his class. There were numerous objections to yard duty assignments, oversize classes, low pay, lack of suitable classroom materials, and parking difficulties. Though it had been only a few days, it seemed as if school had been in session for weeks.

I had received no textbooks or other materials for the children. When I inquired about this, I was told that the "better" classes are taken care of first—"Your children can't read anyway." It was clear to me early that I would have to do what I could with the children on my own. But I was only groping for a way, not having taught before and not having attained as yet any major insights into how teaching must proceed. I had little control with the children, who seemed to have accepted failure as routine. They appeared to expect very little from me, and this was no doubt so because I did not know how to help them. Our room was tucked away on the top floor of Harlem School, and no one seemed to care about us. It was quite apparent that Opportunity Classes were the mark of failure, to be kept out of sight and out of everyone's way. If I would be willing to last it out with Op-5, the administration would be satisfied.

HELP ARRIVES

After several weeks had gone by, Harlem School had settled into routine patterns of behavior. Though I felt less strange on the job, I did not feel competent, nor could I relinquish the memory of one of my earliest experiences at failure and anger. It was a lesson in outrage delivered by another teacher. In the very first week of classes Mr. Messing unexpectedly came to my classroom.

Room 515 was located near a teachers' bathroom and the gymnasium. Thus, the only time it was relatively quiet in our location was in the early morning or during lunch hour. Otherwise the constant bouncing of basketballs and flushings of the toilet provided the sound backdrop to our lessons. On emerging from the teachers' bathroom during the morning in question, Mr. Messing, who had come from down the hall to have a cigarette, stopped to offer his greetings before returning to his own classroom. The children were just coming in and getting seated. He asked me how I was doing, and I confessed that I needed considerably more time before I would feel of service to the children. He smiled knowingly; he had been at Harlem School for nine years and was considered a veteran teacher. He told me that all teachers undergo "beginner's pains" and that I would be all right after a time.

"Here, let me show you how to do it," he said. He looked around the room and picked out Manuel, who was seated in the front row comparing pencil points with another boy. "Hey you, come here!" shouted Mr. Messing. I watched with interest, thinking I would pick up a trick of the trade.

Manuel came forth, smiling. As he approached, Mr. Messing, without warning, struck him full force with an open hand across the face and neck, shouting: "How dare you speak while your teacher and I are talking. Don't ever let me catch you doing that again. Now sit down and keep your big mouth shut. If I catch you doing that again, you'll really be in trouble."

Manuel fought back the tears and returned to his seat in great embarrassment. The other children stared at Mr. Messing. He walked out of the room and I followed him. I asked if he had known Manuel from some previous experience or if he were punishing him for something I should know about. "I don't know him," said Mr. Messing. "But that's the only thing the little bastards understand. He won't give you any more trouble." And he walked off to his own classroom.

As of that time I had had no trouble with Manuel. In fact, he turned out to be one of the quietest, most unassuming children in Op-5. He liked to draw, and he avoided attention. He bothered no one. No matter how I tried to reach him after that incident, Manuel rarely spoke to me at all. It did not serve to tell him that I had denounced Mr. Messing for his action. Manuel did not see me as any different from Mr. Messing. There was no reason for him to trust me or to like me.

4 / "Everybody's been hit by a car"

EVENTUALLY I GOT to know the children in Opportunity Class better. Each child was in many ways unique. Each had a personal history that was interesting and sometimes poignant. Rosa sat in class and smiled at all I said, rarely understanding what I said. On occasion when I thought of the appropriate words in Spanish, she would come alive and look around at the other children, as if she were now an important part of the group too.

Manuel sat and quietly drew pictures in his notebook, carefully scrutinizing his pencils, observing me guardedly, constantly reminded of his encounter with Mr. Messing.

Theodore and Katherine tried as hard as they were able to do all the work they could. Both were orphans who had been reared in the south. Neither had ever had a white teacher before this, and they appeared reserved and cautious in their behavior.

Bernard was a tough kid who had been seen smoking several times, even at this early age. And Vernon, also age ten, with whom Bernard hung out when school was not in session, practiced his shadowboxing whenever class time permitted.

Yolanda translated for Rosa as best she could and often seemed lonely when Rosa was not in class. It was important for Yolanda to be able to speak Spanish in class, though she was fluent in English.

Every child had a distinguishable temperament and personal style. Though I do not mean to depict each child in Op-5 in a simple phrase or two, I do mean to indicate that each could be seen as a particular representation of his cultural experience. The similarities and differences among them had to be seen against that experience even if it were hard to probe beyond that which was manifest in the classroom. But much could be learned, however inadvertently. In fact, Courtney was one child who could have taught all his teachers much, were they to have observed and listened.

Courtney was an identical twin whose brother was in class 5-1. Because there was nothing discernibly "defective" about Courtney, I puzzled over the fact that he was on the "last" class roster in fifth grade while his brother was in the "first" class. Presumably as identical twins the two were of the same genetic material. Why the disparity in class placement? Nothing in the record indicated illness or any other circumstance which would have caused

Courtney any learning disadvantage. In fact, he was without question the best reader and "all-around" student in Op-5.

I asked Courtney, when I discovered that he had a brother in class 5-1, how each of them was placed in classes in the past. He told me that he had been separated from his brother in kindergarten so that teachers would have no difficulty with identification of the two. Over the years Courtney simply ended up in the Opportunity Classes. Soon thereafter he came to be known as a behavior problem. He was not a problem in Op-5; on the contrary, he was exceedingly sharp and always aware of my actions and thoughts. He seemed to sit back and survey all that transpired. I had always suspected that it was he who stuffed the water fountain spout with chewing gum so it would splash the walls when turned on.

There were two other incidents, however, that really indicated Courtney's insights into the system at Harlem School. He continually came to school without a pencil. Each day I gave him one to work with, but it was gone by day's end. He never knew what happened to the many pencils he received. If he did not do homework, it was because he had no pencil, he would inform me. Finally I told him that I could not imagine that he would not have a pencil at home. He assured me that he did not. Some days later he brought a note, ostensibly from home, which verified that "Courtney have no pencil at home." It was signed "his Aunt" and was written in crayon on brown bag paper. I knew I had been outwitted. He had manufactured a note from home and made sure to use crayon to "prove" he had no pencil. Finally I gave him a new mechanical pencil which he safeguarded and brought to school each day. It was a gift well earned, I thought.

Some weeks later Courtney administered a lesson to all of us; it was during the weekly assembly period one afternoon. Presumably this weekly get-together was to serve to bind all the children in common orientation and to allow the reassertion of prevailing attitudes about school, education, and nation.[1] Each child was to wear a white shirt or blouse to commemorate the ritual. To encourage children in this purpose, classes in which all wore white shirts were given "commendation cards." Courtney never wore a white shirt, seemingly delighting in "spoiling it" for the others in the class and grade.[2] The leader of the assembly would admonish Courtney continually for depriving the entire grade of "one hundred per cent white shirts," and she would berate him publicly. When out of curiosity I asked him why he did not wear a white shirt, he said that there was only one white shirt at home and that his brother got to wear that one. Whether he was telling the truth or not, I thought his answer was more than adequate.

---

[1] See Honigmann (1963:171–176). The author gives a succinct explanation of rites of intensification.

[2] James Baldwin explains that "you wore a white shirt to school to prove, again, that you were not a nigger." Others, too, object to the connotation of making it mandatory that children wear white shirts to school. See *My Childhood*, a Metromedia Film depicting James Baldwin's Harlem childhood.

On one of these assembly period days Courtney was at first not present. The period began at 1:15 and usually ended about 2:15 in the afternoon. Children marched in and participated in the opening exercises: The Pledge of Allegiance, "The Star-Spangled Banner," and a hymn. This was to be followed by a passage from the Bible, when Courtney came marching in. It was now 1:30. The teacher who was reading from the Bible halted and addressed Courtney, "Where do you think you're going, young man? You can't just wander in here whenever you feel like it. Whose child is he?" I acknowledged that he was "mine." But Courtney spoke for himself: "I went to get Big Maybelle," he said.

"Who is Big Maybelle?" asked the assembly leader.

"She's a singer."

"So what."

"She could entertain us."

"Who asked you to get her?"

"Nobody. I did it myself."

"Is she coming?"

"I don't know."

Courtney was directed to his seat while the preliminary proceedings were concluded. The entire assembly then waited for Big Maybelle to show up. At 2:30 in the afternoon it was apparent that no one was coming to entertain us. In fact, it was Courtney who had provided the entertainment. I asked him later if there were a Big Maybelle. He said that he thought there was, but that he did not know her in any case.

At first I thought that I had attributed too much to this incident, but I came to believe with conviction that Courtney had made up the entire story simply to excuse his lateness that afternoon. Furthermore, I think he knew that no one would mind his act. By keeping classes in the auditorium until 2:30 he made us "kill" the entire afternoon. At Harlem School few teachers lingered at the end of a day. It was customary to vacate the buildings as quickly as possible. All seemed anxious to "escape." Some teachers knew the subway schedule perfectly, making sure not to miss a particular train at a precise time. In delaying us, Courtney had in effect brought the day to a close. It would not pay to begin new lessons that late in the afternoon. He was doing everyone a favor. He clearly knew that a permissible cause to avoid instruction eased things for teachers and children. To me it was another thought-out gambit to repay us at Harlem School. If Courtney was going to be in a "dumb" class, he would wholly convince us just how "dumb" he was.

Courtney was not the only child from whom one could learn. Kenny was another bright child who was one step ahead of me at every turn. Indeed, it was he who so skillfully wielded the window pole on our first day of class. He was sturdy and smart. He was also compellingly attractive, with many winning ways. I liked him, and he knew it. It was his behavior that eventually provided me with a major insight into children's behavior in general at Harlem School.

Children were to arrive for afternoon sessions at Harlem School by 12:50. One afternoon Kenny appeared instead at 2 P.M. I asked why he was late, and he said he had been hitching rides on the backs of buses. It was quite apparent that he had also taken a haircut since the morning session. I assumed that that was really why he was late. Nevertheless, Kenny got lost in thoughts about buses and suddenly asked me, "Hey, teacher, you ever been hit by a car?" I said I had not, in response to which he said, "Aw, don't gimme that shit!"[3] He did not mean to shock; he tried to catch himself, but the words came. He could not help it. He really believed it was improbable that I had never been hit by a car. "Everybody's been hit by a car at least once," he said.

Soon the children began to warm up to Kenny's antics. They had begun to "sound."[4] They were most appreciative of his daring confrontation with me. Kenny realized this and refused my invitation to be seated and join the rest of the class. He remained at the back of the room and dared: "If you want me, come and get me."

Hardly in anger, but without warning, I sprung after him. Shocked, he ran down the hallway and into the gym, but I caught him before he could get out the other side. Quickly he tried to explain away his capture: "The only reason you caught me," he said, "is because I ain't wearing my sneakers." "Neither am I," I responded. I had no time to think of a better answer. But it seemed to suffice, for Kenny relented and quietly walked back with me to the classroom. He sat down and remained silent for the remainder of the day. The children too seemed surprised.

I noticed after a few weeks that Kenny and I were not as much of a problem, one to the other, as heretofore. I did not know why this was so, but we had begun to see one another differently and perhaps more positively as well. It puzzled me, though I approved of our new condition, and I wanted to figure it out. I knew that I was not teaching him any better, necessarily, but Kenny obviously had gained a measure of respect for me. An occurrence on a Friday afternoon helped me finally to put things into perspective. Again it was quite coincidental.

I was late getting out of the building after school and I found I could not start my car. Everyone had gone except Mr. Norman. I spotted him and asked if he would help me in trying to start my car on a push. We tried, but with no success. Before long, a veritable parade of persons came by to suggest remedies for my dilemma.

"Hey, fella, do you have gas in the car?"

---

[3] Children often use colloquialisms as extensions of normal speech. This language is frequently expressive and relevant. See, for example, *Play it Cool in English*, Riessman and Dawkins, eds. (1967).

[4] See Burley (1966:119–121). The author explains the origin of verbal assault by field slaves against the favored house servants during the period of slavery. He traces the historic course of this pattern through the jazz idiom and Negro subculture. "Sounding," the constant denigration of one another and the other's family, as manifest by Harlem School children, may be a variant of this pattern. This form of "bring down" is not new in other ethnic groups as well.

"It's probably the fuel pump."

"No, it's gotta be the spark plugs."

"I think it's the points."

On and on it went; almost every youth or adult male in the vicinity offered a cause and a remedy for my problem. Eventually a mechanic from a neighboring service station started the car for me, but the incident lingered in my mind. I had even noted that subsequent passersby had argued with previous passersby when most had not even bothered to check the car's engine or anything else. Oratory seemed primary (Liebow 1967:163); the topic was secondary. I realized that each corner was an assembly point for argument and debate, for greeting others and watching neighborhood events. A stalled car was a subject for discussion, each protagonist trying to assert his own verbal expertise.

In the months I had now spent at Harlem School, it had become evident that children also put high value on debate and physical prowess. Almost every girl was an expert rope jumper, irrespective of her classroom performance. Even this had its vocal aspects—the girls chanting rhythmic verses as they bounded up and down. And every boy, with few exceptions, was adept at defending a point either orally or by assuming a boxer's stance if he had to. In putting it all together—my stalled car, my reading, and my chase after Kenny—I could now understand my new relationship to Kenny. Inadvertently I had exhibited two important attributes of his cultural existence when I had caught him in the gym. For one thing I did outrun him and catch him. Secondly I outquipped him when he told me he had been caught because he was without his sneakers and I had answered that I was also without mine. He could not know that my response was without forethought. He had assumed a more amenable posture in the classroom because it appeared to him that I had met him on his own terms. Thus, if I could behave within his "rules," he would try to live within mine. Ours was now a relationship that was reciprocal, not the previous one-way relationship that had existed. Hopefully, I thought, it was no longer teacher *to* child, but teacher *and* child. It was almost as if I had been hit by a car. Kenny liked that. If I could run after him and catch him, he could pay attention in class—just in case there might be something there that he should know.

5 / Culture and education:
the teacher as fieldworker

I HAD TRIED HARD to get to know the children in Opportunity Class. They had many talents, and I wanted to translate and adapt these to the classroom setting. No other help was forthcoming. Administrators preoccupied themselves with chores relating to the distribution of materials and supplies. They did not find it equally imperative to assist new teachers in the instruction of children. Perhaps this was just as well. I do not believe that the children in Op-5 were liked very much by school officials. Courtney and Kenny, for example, were not acquiescent as were some other children. They could not uncritically accept everything teachers said. They did not conform to the docile, obedient image consistently held out to them. I thought that if I were left alone, unimpeded by trivial school tasks, I would eventually be able to work well with the children. Going it alone at Harlem School seemed to be the normal pattern anyway. In addition, I had grown scornful of the customary hitting of children. Teachers spoke about it at lunchtime, and one could observe daily instances of such procedures. Many reasons were given in attempts to support this practice.

"When you hit a kid, he at least feels that you care about him. It's better than simply disregarding him."

"Look, these kids are beaten at home all the time. They're always fighting with each other, aren't they? It's something they are used to and understand."

"You have to hit your own kids at home, right?"

"Their parents expect us to straighten them out. Otherwise they would complain. But they don't."

Some teachers even complained about not being able to hit the very young children because they were too small. "But they are the ones who really need it," they said. "Then maybe they wouldn't be so wild when they got into the upper grades."

Curiously, no teacher submitted that his or her class was entirely free of "problem" children, despite the harsh controlling practices advocated and employed. And though I knew there were teachers who felt no need of such oppressive measures, who sought to give the best instruction without resorting to punitive devices, there was little opportunity to discuss alternative approaches with them. The lunch period was the only time during the school day when teachers had a chance to get together. One still had to forge his own way, to avoid the sense of helplessness and even hopelessness at Harlem School. Although some teachers wanted their children to do well, they did not really expect it to happen. So many took defeat as normal.

> For his own mental health, the teacher learns not to care. The job is just too frustrating, and more difficult than any job has a right to be. He has to battle both students and supervisors. He sees no tangible results . . . and feels no sense of accomplishment. He has little identification with or loyalty to the school since he does not participate in policy or share the rewards of the school's accomplishment—his supervisors decide almost everything and take almost all the credit. Thus initiated into the profession, and now a hardened cynic, he, too, asserts, "the kids cannot learn," and under the circumstances it is probably true (Ornstein 1967:49).

I realized it would be too easy to succumb to this behavioral style. I wanted to draw back and view what was happening at Harlem School with a more detached eye. I knew that behavior could not always be understood by its overt manifestations alone. Things could not be seen in isolation, apart from grosser cultural patterns. I had to learn to examine "the cultural influences shaping the role of the child" (Kimball 1963: 268–283), and to see Harlem School as a social system—a semi-autonomous institution that had roots in the local community and in the communities from which the teachers came each day. I had to see that each classroom itself was a culture system inter-related with other cultural systems. And it was the interplay of these with the covert personalities of the children that might make events meaningful and comprehensible.

Several occurrences did subsequently take place which revealed implicit bases for children's behavior. Certainly it did not suffice to accept at face value that the children failed to succeed in school because they were "under-privileged" or "culturally deprived" (Mackler and Giddings 1965:608–613). There had to be alternative explanations.

While on lunchroom yard duty one afternoon, I was joined by Mr. Young, the only black male teacher on the faculty at Harlem School. We spoke casually and informally when Mr. Dorf approached. He greeted us and then entered the cafeteria where the children had gathered in the usual long lines for their lunch. Most of the children at Harlem School participated in the "free lunch" program, arranged for children from families on welfare or of low income. Mr. Dorf soon returned, apparently disgruntled. "The nerve of these women," he said. "They wouldn't give me anything to eat until the kids were finished." He seemed even more angry as he told us about it. "The damn kids don't even eat the food. Look at them throwing it all over the place. I at least eat it. They don't appreciate it." He then told us that he usually goes out for lunch, but he did not feel like doing so that day.

The neighborhood women who worked in the children's cafeteria had a difficult job feeding hundreds of children at lunch time, and they had asked Mr. Dorf to wait until all had been served before he asked for his own food. In fact, they had requested in the past that he send a note beforehand, informing them that he preferred lunch. They would then prepare it for him and have it sent to his room. The price was 45 cents. This had not appeased him, however. He felt that he had been discourteously treated. Mr. Young listened and then addressed himself to Mr. Dorf.

> You think the children are ungrateful. That's not the case; and it isn't that they aren't hungry. That's not why they throw some of the food away. They know better than anyone else what hunger means. Have you ever been to some of these kids' homes? Do you know what it means to live in a railroad flat, where there is no real kitchen? It's just a room with a sink and stove, but it is also a bedroom at night and a living room during the day. Sometimes, it's big enough to hold only two chairs and a small table. I know what it's like. You have to eat in shifts; if you happen to be last one night, you might not get much to eat. They know what it means to be hungry. Don't fool yourself.
>
> I'll tell you something else. A lot of these kids sleep with towels dipped in turpentine around their heads to keep the rats away at night. The rats are hungry, too. You know that mothers sometimes leave crumbs in corners so the rats will go for that and not for the kids who might have gone to bed with food dried on their faces. You can see dozens of kids in this school who have been bitten by rats.
>
> You know, these are kids who have been on welfare. They've heard all kinds of stories about handouts and breadlines. They don't always get turkey at Thanksgiving or Christmas. You see them eating pickles and gum in class all the time. It isn't that their parents don't care, either; they don't always have more. On top of this, the kids see television and they look at magazines. They've seen what a four course meal looks like. They would like to get that in school themselves. If they throw food away, or you think they do, it's because they don't like the way it's presented to them. You don't eat soup as a main dish, do you? Or peanut butter? They don't want it either, even if it might be healthy for them.
>
> You see, you think of food the way your parents might have taught you; you know: "Don't waste food because the people in Europe are starving." Well, these kids have certain attitudes about food, too. They aren't crazy about handouts. They would prefer a hero sandwich over at the East Side, but they don't have the money. It's like a guy who drinks beer wherever he goes because he grew up in a poor neighborhood and never heard of a mixed drink. Some kids prefer hamburger because they never heard of filet mignon.

The lesson was unplanned, but it was pointed. Both Mr. Dorf and I listened carefully to Mr. Young's explanation. It was a pertinent example of understanding behavior "beneath the surface." I was able then to recall examples from my own childhood where children of families on "relief" refused to wear the mackinaws they received because it stamped them as poor and needy. Each coat had the same plaid design, making children recognizable to those not on "relief."

I realized much more clearly that one had to discern the strategies children had adopted to respond to the school's denigrating posture. If they were described as stupid, they would find ways of bringing their "stupidity" to bear. It was not hard for them to decode the disguises the school had in depicting them. For example, the reading level of a science book would be indicated by the number of footprints on the binding. Op-5 knew quite well that two footprints meant that their book was on a second grade level. This symbol, I learned, contributed to their "inability" (unwillingness) to read.

It was simply too demeaning. They were fifth-graders, and they did not want to read a second-grade book. It would have been just as easy to put five foot-prints on the same book, but no one had thought of that. Children's confidence might then have been built. Instead, it waned more the longer they were in school. Indeed, children's achievements only mirrored teachers' expectations of them (Hechinger 1967:E9).

There were many stereotypes harbored by teachers and administrators at Harlem School. I began to wonder to what extent these attitudes, however unfounded, contributed to the very behavior of children so energetically denounced by school officials.

> There are those who expect children to come to school with capabilities limited only by their innate potential. Some who hold this position believe that when children do not achieve in school it is because of limitations in this innate potential. When they discover that the largest proportion of underachievers comes from lower socio-economic groups and from various racial and ethnic groups, they label these groups innately inferior. While there might not always be a conscious recognition of this perception, their expectations for performance are significantly different with regard to children from less favored groups. That means if they are teachers, the job demands they make on themselves may be determined by these prejudices. Further, the demands they make on the children are consistent with these perceptions . . . and the children . . . respond accordingly (Deutsch 1962:14–15).

But what are the results when teachers and children misinterpret one another's intentions? Teachers spoke of instilling fear in the children, and this became for many an instrument of pedagogy. Yet, it seemed to be such an uncomfortable philosophy to live with. A peculiar paranoia pervaded Harlem School, and it was unreasonable not to expect the children to react (Henry 1966:137–145). "Those deny the world whom the world denies" (Kimball and McClellan 1962:235).

> What happens to a dream deferred?
>   Does it dry up
>   like a raisin in the sun
>   Or fester like a sore—
>   And then run?
>
>   Does it stink like rotten meat?
>   Or crust and sugar over—
>   like a syrupy sweet?
>   Maybe it just sags
>   like a heavy load.
>
>   Or does it explode?
>   (Hughes 1963:67–68)

THE CULTURE OF HARLEM SCHOOL

My life with Op-5 was a short-lived one. At midyear I was assigned to another class. Maternity leave had been granted to a teacher in the fifth grade, and I was being asked to take over her class. I protested. I had struggled to gain deeper insights into the children, and I felt it unfair to relinquish my growing attachment to them. My protest was disallowed. "You ought to be glad to get rid of them," Mr. Green said. "They would drive you crazy." But I was not happy to be rid of them, particularly when I learned they would not be getting a new teacher of their own. Instead, the children were to be redistributed among other classes in the fifth grade, two children to each class. None of them would be in my new fifth-grade class. Besides, placement would be made according to children's reading levels. This meant that Rosa, who spoke so little English, would be separated from Yolanda, who had enjoyed translating for her in Op-5. The procedure just seemed to mark another failure for the children. No doubt they felt they had once again been abandoned. When I asked if the other fifth-grade class could be given a new teacher and I be permitted to remain with Op-5, I was told: "Your children can't learn anything anyway. What do they need a teacher for?"

On our last day together, before the shift to the new classes, I told the children that I hoped they would do well in their new classes. Somehow, I hoped, they would make it. But in fact, I knew they would not. The system weighed too heavily upon them. I wondered too if I would escape its imprint. The only way, I felt, to avoid being rendered ineffective and distant was to set about deliberately understanding the cultural and social patterning at Harlem School. Perhaps one could beat the system by better knowing it.

Every school is in some way like a small society. The members of the group are enjoined in a system of constraints and allowances which regulates the behavior of each of them. A prevailing culture or life style exists. People come together in interactional patterns from which mannerisms and beliefs are derived. Perceptions are built and balanced against the perceptions others have of you. People can be numbered and described, as can the places in which they assemble and disperse. And particular events give insight into the organizational pattern and the division of labor among those coming together. Thus, regularities of behavior become known; an order and sequence of events is discerned. All of this was shaping itself in my mind. After an initial period of "adjustment" I thought I would soon be able to work consciously and deliberately to reverse the pattern of failure, at least among some children. I knew, however, that much more had to be known about the school.

The school also provides a physical environment within which people interact. Everyone knows what schools look like in general. Rows of desks and blackboards hung on walls immediately give indication of the kinds of activities that take place in such a surrounding. Similarly there are material means by which the environment is exploited; a technology exists consisting of books, papers, chalk, and other learning equipment. Some of this material inventory may be reserved for particular places in the physical environment, so, for example, record cards are kept in offices and basketballs are for use in gyms, and so on. A dispersal pattern emerges whereby things and persons are placed in ordered ways. Thus, theoretically, libraries are not placed near gyms in order that noise levels be kept low when persons privately read.

There is a school population too. Harlem School houses children of particular ages only, and further subdivisions and groupings of agemates are ordered on the bases of skill and compatibility. Sequential progressions through the school life cycle are provided for, so that at different ages children are to assume different skills and knowledge. Teachers act as the sponsors and priests in the system, and it is against their standards that children must measure up. Thus, in their custody at Harlem School were approximately 1,800 children, aged six to twelve. More than 90 percent of this student population were black, while 80 percent of the teachers were white. The feelings about this "color breakdown" also played a part in the interpretation of Harlem School activities, even if they remained covert for the most part.

The school organizational pattern resulted, in a formal sense, from the application of the school's technology on the school environment by the persons existing in it. A system of rank and status grows out in which certain persons hold sway over others. Preference is exerted by those vested with such power, the children generally being subordinate in the formal structure. It is expected, therefore, that teachers will initiate activities for children and not the reverse. In turn, teachers are to be responsible to still others higher in the order—principal and supervisors. Some activities may be reserved for children in the same class, while others might be for an entire group of agemates; for example, assemblies. Still other endeavors are for individuals: getting a drink of water, sharpening one's pencil, or being a monitor.

All of this is made possible of course by the unique inheritance of all people —the ability to use language and other forms of symbolic communication. Children draw, they read, sing songs, and daydream; teachers gesture, exhort, encourage, reward, and punish. There grows out a system of sentiments and morality. There are appropriate forms of address and appropriate styles of clothing. These all contribute to the symbolic and "religious" system of the school. A gold star is to be approved. A red mark means danger in the learning life of the child.

The result of the fusion of all these subsystems is an intermeshing of people, things, and thoughts. Children are expected to leave Harlem School upon graduation, having been substantially altered in mind from what they were when they entered school at the start. It is curious, however, that a similar transformation is not expected of the teacher, although it is hoped that he will sharpen and increase his skills in working with children.

Each class of children also forms a separate culture system with its own physical and social boundaries. Categorically, a child may be a fifth-grader, let us say, but the class of children in which he participates daily involves him in a particular relational system which may be rather different from other relational systems on the grade. He may share common orientations and even experiences with others across the grade, but his in-class experience may be unique to him alone. Thus, one must look at the overall social system and the individual culture systems to best estimate the child's experience in school.

At Harlem School there was, in addition, a characteristic and prevailing ethos by which all activities were defined and given meaning. It was a behavioral disposition that spelled discontent and abrasion among its population. Not one teacher would really depict his place of work as congenial or as a place where anticipations were fulfilled. Indeed, the reactions of the children suggested that they did not find it a happy place either.

It is of critical importance to note this, I think, because most schools in New York City have similar inventories of material goods and teaching staffs with collective experiences similar to those of the staff at Harlem School. The ordering of activities is likewise standard and familiar. Are other schools unhappy places for children? Why do teachers remain at Harlem School while others leave? Were different children housed in Harlem School, would things be different? There were many questions that a research posture suggested, and many answers could be sought in many places. But Harlem School itself held the key to any explanation of what went on within it.

A CHANGE AGENT

My new class was an "average" fifth-grade group. At Harlem School "average" classes were not as far behind in achievement as "below average" classes, but they were below expected standards, nevertheless. With this group too I soon realized that school conditions, more than anything else, contributed to their underachievement. Teachers had expected little from the children and had given them little in return. There were curriculum guides that teachers were to follow, but each class really went off on its own, molded in a style that primarily reflected the teacher's own temperament and character. Subject matter was not central. What seemed uppermost was the drive to limit children's overt responses. I had learned that a "good" teacher at Harlem School was one who controlled his classes well. Had they been well instructed as a result, this was simply a fortuitous by-product.

By the time I got to know the thirty-four children in my new class, it was time to prepare them for their next class, for before long the conditioning process to enter their records for the next school year had begun. By May of that first school year most teachers acted as if the long haul were nearly over. There was a lot of busy work, drawing pictures, and the like. If my class had learned anything significant, it was largely through good fortune, not expert instruction. If nothing more, however, I was now assuming a new role. Things that seemed theoretical outside the classroom became quite real inside it. Immediate responses had to be called forth so often, yet I had also to dispassionately assess the legitimacy and adequacy of the procedures and techniques I selected. I had come to see the teaching task as a research task as well. School is where the children are, and the teacher must systematically share their lifeways. It is not a contrived situation. It is normal for teachers to be in schools, and one need not be seen as an outsider. Of course the teacher must still win the confidence of those he works with, as does the field researcher;

and he must prove his own humanity while he probes the qualities present in the children. It is an interesting role, for it allows the teacher as participant-observer to define his task as he fulfills it. And if the field situation itself suggests items for future study, all that was occurring now appeared to be a stimulus for further understanding.

> The regularities of the social world are comprehensible—their apparent opaqueness being in reality a creation of our own ignorance. The acquisition of competence in social relations lies within the grasp of all, but only as there are structures which give the relations expression.
> If the problems which confront us today are to be solved they must be met at the level where they occur and by those who are involved (Kimball and Pearsall 1954:xxiii).

The need to see teachers and children forming a joint social structure was paramount. As data were accumulated and perceptions derived therefrom, they could be turned into meaningful educational and scientific problems (Thompson 1965:280). Why did children underachieve? What was the contribution of the teacher to this process? More and more I was confirmed in my view that anthropology as a discipline was well suited toward helping me understand education at Harlem School. There are thousands of culture systems throughout the world in which a variety of means are employed to convey the cultural heritage to children so that they acquire and internalize the skills and central beliefs necessary for participation in their societies (Henry 1960: 267–305). Study of these diverse cultures has given the insight that children are capable of numerous and varied responses to cultural stimuli (Mead and Wolfensten 1955). What children become is, in essence, what the parental generation strives to make them become. Childhood is definable in terms of adults' perceptions. It was school people who gave children at Harlem School a perception of themselves, and this very definition worked toward prescribing the kinds of learning activities in which the children participated.

> In its broadest sense, education is the cultural process, the way in which each newborn human infant, born with a potentiality for learning greater than that of any other mammal, is transformed into a full member of a specific human society, sharing with the other members a specific human culture. From this point of view we can place side by side the newborn child in a modern city and the . . . infant born into some primitive South Sea tribe. Both have everything to learn. Both depend for that learning upon the help and example, the care and tutelage, of the elders of their societies.[2]

At Harlem School the prevailing feeling was that the failure of children in class was mostly the result of forces outside the school and outside the control of educators. Either the family was at the root of failure, or something (usually intangible) within the child himself. Little attention was directed toward the organizational and attitudinal patterns within the school. A certain number of failures among students was perennially anticipated. The fact that I, an inex-

---

[2] Mead (1964:162). This material is from "Our Educational Emphases in Primitive Prospective," a selection in Dr. Mead's compiled writings.

perienced teacher, was placed with an Opportunity Class, a very questionable appointment, was indicative of this view. If children could not learn, it was thought, why waste an experienced teacher on them? But this thinking needs reexamination. Here too the ethic of anthropology is related.

> "The science of culture," concluded Tylor, "is essentially a reformer's science." I would suggest that anthropology is something more—a revolutionary discipline. This does not make anthropology any the less a science; on the contrary, it is more fully a science precisely because it strives toward a more spacious form of knowing, of "sciencing," and is, therefore, a most potent tool for cultural criticism. . . .
> The anthropological habit of mind is synthetic, not merely analytic: it looks for wholes, patterns, processes, and relationships among various aspects of culture and between cultures, and it ferrets out and examines cultural first assumptions (Diamond 1964:432).

There are, of course, problems involved in studying cultural process. This was true at Harlem School. Not every observer sees the same things, even when looking at the same things (Foster 1961–1962:174–178). The same problem may be defined and interpreted differently by different persons. One must first have an objective sense of his own relationship to the observed (L. Bohannan 1966:28–33). And this is sometimes aided by objective study; in examining the cultural milieu at Harlem School the teacher might not emerge as a better teacher, but he will certainly come to know why this is so. Reasonably one would expect that an intimate knowledge of the children's lifeways and the neighborhood surroundings would have implication for teaching style and instructional procedure, a result that itself is worth the fervent efforts of the teacher because it broadens and makes more relevant his technical equipment.

> The goal is to examine the dynamics of human beings in interaction, living within a habitat or given type of environment. The habitat includes not only the physical items of that environment but also other persons and the prevailing moral and ethical codes. . . . In addition . . . constituent groups possess a past, are repetitive in their organization and activities, exhibit an internal equilibrium, and thus yield to methods of systematic analysis (Kimball 1955a:65).

"YOUR JOB IS TO TEACH HIM, NOT SMELL HIM"

It ought to be clear that there are some additional difficulties when the teacher assumes the role of researcher. In the normal instance the ethnographer is responsible to the host culture and to the collectivity making up the discipline he purportedly represents. He is also responsible for the uses to which he puts his findings. He must be "chary of accepting extant data as adequate, since all too often they have been compiled for quite other purposes and likely carry incrustations of irrelevant assumptions (Kimball 1955b:1137).

At Harlem School I felt my responsibility to be to the children (and their parents) and to fellow teachers. The use to which professional educators put new found knowledge is often to programs for the future. Parents, on the other hand, are understandably more interested in demonstrable and more immediate results; that is, they want the best possible education for their children, realizing well that what their children learn in school is certainly related to life's chances and what they may become in the future. Postponement of better education diminishes the personal opportunities for which that education would have been prerequisite.

An interesting and amusing story was told by teachers at Harlem School which was related to this concern. It was no doubt part of the folklore that comes out of educational institutions. The story told of a teacher who noted that a child in his class continually wore the same clothing without a change. This went on for several weeks, so that allegedly other children in the class had begun to ridicule the child and to say that he "smelled." Finally the teacher sent a note home with the boy in question, politely suggesting to the parent that the child be given a change of clothing because "the other children were making fun of him and saying that he smelled." The mother of the child, as the story went, wrote a return note to the teacher in which she said: "Your job is to teach him, not smell him."

One might also assert that it is not the teacher's job to preoccupy himself in gathering knowledge through research, for as he is getting his variables in order he may be neglecting the children. Indeed, it was the dominant view at Harlem School that teachers were so pressed by the immediacy of classroom management and instruction that they had no time for research or experiment. I would deny that one can not learn through research and teach at the same time. I would say that one must learn as he teaches. The real moral problem in probing the cultural atmosphere at Harlem School which people wanted to avoid was that they might discover insights and facts that would prompt them to heretofore uncontemplated action; that is, the results of inquiry might lead some to a revisionist or reform point of view that does not meet prevalent consensus. In short, to know is not necessarily to understand; and to understand is not necessarily to act in an informed and committed way.[3] Furthermore, what one learns from his involvement with others may reveal a situation he did not know to exist before and which is at odds with his original intentions for getting involved in the situation in the first place (Turnbull 1966: 8–14). This knowledge may serve as a spur to entire new habits of mind and action. Sometimes these actions are such that the individual did not perceive that he was capable of them (see Kozol 1967).

These theoretical concerns are sometimes not seemingly as important as the more overt and direct effects on teachers of being in the new cultural setting. Many teachers at Harlem School confessed a feeling of "strangeness" at the school. Of the entire staff only nine teachers were non-white. Virtually no permanent friendships existed between black and white teachers, and even the informal lunchroom talk fests revealed white and black teachers to be aloof from one another. Some white teachers attributed the lack of response in the children as based in anti-white feelings. And some of the black teachers con-

---

[3] See Bowen (1964). The author describes the difficulty in trying to behave in a foreign culture by the ethical guidelines of one's own culture.

cluded that the failure of children to learn was grounded in anti-black feelings among white teachers. These feelings were a microcosmic reflection of the larger societal macrocosm where similar reactions are engendered. But they may also have been a partial reaction to the culture shock that many teachers undergo. Finding their usual perceptions tenuous, they seek alternative explanations for their feelings of discomfort. Some are able to overcome this quickly; others never fully recover or escape its influence, even if they are not consciously aware of this. I was convinced that the hitting of children so manifest at Harlem School was one variation of the culture shock syndrome. Teachers' frustrations in not being able to communicate more readily and effectively with children rendered them angry and disappointed. For many it was easier to blame and assess children the penalties for these feelings.

A teacher might strike out often enough at children so that he came eventually to lend a rationale and support to the procedure. In some instances such a teacher would not approve such behavior in others, yet his anxiety and sense of defenselessness in the classroom made him accept such measures in the hope that they were only temporary. Such a teacher, in culture shock, had to be made to "recognize it for what it is—a temporary attitude that will pass as soon as he becomes familiar enough with . . . local customs and manners that at least some of them will be predictable. The only cure . . . is a forced-draft, purposeful pushing on ahead. The way to get over it is to work at making new persons and new ways familiar and known" (Arensberg and Niehoff 1964: 189).

This kind of immersion in the new setting of Harlem School was for me an awakening after my first year of teaching. I saw the school as an encampment within the dominant culture where the same drama was played out between the poor and those who regulate their lives. "We do not give the same kind of food, clothing, housing, medical care, recreation, or justice to the deprived children that we give to those in comfortably-well-off homes. We don't like to think of class distinctions in American life, so we tend to shy away from these unacceptable facts."[4] But one could not shy away from these facts at Harlem School; each day on the children's faces one unmistakably saw the effects of poverty and miseducation. This awareness could not easily be relinquished, despite the efforts of those who tried.

---

[4] Goodwin Watson in the preface to *The Culturally Deprived Child*, Riessman (1962:ix).

6 / Reading, writing, 'rithmetic, rats, and roaches: school and community

ARLEM SCHOOL had a particular character to it, its own subculture. However, it existed in a neighborhood setting and the larger Harlem community. I had gained some sense of children's behavior and thoughts, and had observed and experienced the reactions of teachers in my first year. It was necessary also to understand more fully the nature of community life and the relationship of school to community. There is often a discernible pattern even in the idiosyncratic, just as there is often special meaning in the usual. An important question to decide was whether the school and the community represented different subcultures or fused to make one subculture.

Harlem School was opened in 1901. It had served in some way a variety of ethnic groups which had moved out of the neighborhood as new groups came in. The school now had a population of children which was about 92 percent black and 8 percent Puerto Rican. No other ethnic group was really represented, except of course among the professional staff. For most of the children their contact with teachers was their only bridge to the larger, dominant, white culture existing outside the immediate locale. And for the teachers their involvement at Harlem School was the first opportunity for most of them to get a glimpse into the world of the poor and the excluded. Thus, the grosser societal differences in social and economic opportunity existed in microcosm in the school. There was a juxtaposition of the child's world with the teacher's. An indicative instance occurred in Mr. Norman's fifth-grade class.

One day Mr. Norman discovered rats in the classroom. Naturally he wanted to be rid of them. He set traps overnight and found the next day that two rats had been caught. To his surprise he also found that the children cheered his efforts. They volunteered each morning to collect and dump the slaughtered rats in the toilet as the campaign continued. So avid were they in this effort that Mr. Norman hit upon a new discipline technique. He told the children that the "privilege" of disposing of the rats would be given to only those who behaved in class the previous day, did all their work, and came to school on time. For children who at an early age had heard the ominous squeakings of rats in the tenement walls and had come to hate these cunning apartment invaders, it was a privilege they sought to exercise. Thus, they

29

obeyed the rules Mr. Norman set down. In two weeks the rats disappeared, and Mr. Norman delighted in reporting to other teachers that he had had the best discipline ever in his class during this period of the year. The children had responded to his efforts with all the ingenuity of their personal experiences. It had made Mr. Norman a "pied piper" of learning for this brief time.

To be sure, there are innumerable personal and collective attributes brought to the school by the children. These were not always probed, however. Partially it was so because teachers did not know what to look for; and in some instances they did not care, for they were bound to traditional methods from which they could not escape. In seating, for example, the child's sense of space was not taken into account. He was rooted to his seat, just as his seat was rooted to the floor. Even when movable furniture was on hand, teachers recreated the same patterns that existed in classrooms with stationary seats. And a child sat in the same place for every subject matter. If he were seen as a "behavior problem," in addition, he might be placed close to the teacher where he sat for music, art, arithmetic, social studies, and every other subject. The classroom was not arranged to be representative of what was being taught, but geared to the behavioral characteristics of the child as perceived by the teacher. This "imprisonment" did indeed serve to lock out the subject matter too. Subject matter could not be primary within such procedures.

> Although there is considerable inter-teacher variation in classroom atmosphere and in the amount of time devoted to actual subject-teaching, our time samples indicated that as much as 80 percent of the school day was channeled into disciplining, and secondarily, into organizational details such as collecting milk money, cookie funds, special principal reports and the like. . . .
> The implications of this are extremely important. They suggest that the lower-class Negro child receives one-half to one-third the exposure to learning (Deutsch 1960:23).

Harlem School too was ordered around organizational demands, often trivial. It was more important to "take the pass" when one left the room than to adhere to the imperatives of effective classroom instruction. Mr. Hecht often said that it was "more important to keep teachers happy than to cater to children's whims." There was a failure to see that children's feelings are entwined with the feelings of teachers, each depending on the other. And before the child could be engaged in meaningful learning tasks, his subcultural experience would have to be interpreted (Khleif 1966:178). If a child sleeps three in a bed, for example, it is not unlikely that he might like to sit two in a seat. Certainly he might not mind sleeping two in a tent. This does not necessarily mean that he makes a good Boy Scout, but it suggests conceptually that children are used to many ways of doing things in the home and in neighborhood that might manifest themselves in various forms in the classroom. Children's constant movement in the classroom suggested to me that this was the result of living at close quarters at home, mingling with many others in a small apartment. This contrasted somewhat with the usual expectations of middle-class children in the suburbs, who may have their own rooms and be used to isolation in individual seats in class. It is commensurate with such children's home experience. Some rooms are reserved for visiting company, others for formal dining, and still others for playing and rough-housing. This was not often the case for the poor child at Harlem School. His reaction to the spatial outlay of the classroom was often different.

All children have a spatial and temporal sense of the world around them. Though the Harlem child might have a diminished physical space—spending much of his time in the immediate neighborhood—he had an expanded social life-space, seeing hundreds of persons on his block each day; and he interacted with many of them. The suburban child might have an enlarged physical space in which to interact—driving by bus many miles to school, for instance —but he might well have a diminished social life-space, seeing on his street only his agemates, who may be few in number where streets are wide and lawns separate the homes. It was clear to me that I would have to contemplate the Harlem setting more carefully, that I would need to introduce subject matter in class that included items from the children's environment and not only aspects of the larger culture. In this way the relationship of local community to the larger society is more readily seen.[1] What were the peripheries of neighborhood? What was the individual's activity range? Where did the school fit in among his other contacts?

A look at the streets bordering Harlem School told much. There were not the sprawling shopping centers characteristic of the suburbs. There were beauty shops, drugstores, realty and insurance establishments, several churches of different denomination, small eating places, a record shop, a pawn shop, a dime store, fruit stands, candy stores, liquor stores, a funeral home, and the ever-present pushcart of fruits and vegetables. The school appeared sometimes as the place where activity came to a halt. So many things were going on elsewhere: men on corners, women in laundramats, and the daily activities of shopping, chatting, and hanging around told much to the child. He was as much of it as anyone else. Only the teacher seemed detached. Yet, the child was the product of all this, the drama of existence that was played out on all those streets around the school.

> I'm talking now about Harlem: a six square mile festering black scar on the alabaster underbelly of the white man's indifference.
>
> HARLEM: A bastard child, born out of wedlock, baptized in the gut bucket of life, midwifed by oppression and fathered by racial hate, circumscribed by fear and guilt-ridden detractors.
>
> HARLEM: A hot-hearted, generously kind, and jovial black woman, whose blood-sucked veins are a playground, whose skinned and scarred, bruised and battered, used and tattered, seduced and raped body is a privileged sanctuary

---

[1] See Arensberg and Kimball (1965:IX). The authors define community as a "master institution or master social system; a key to society; . . . a main link, perhaps a major determinant, in the connections between culture and society."

for that unholy trinity of rent gouging landlords, graft grabbing cops, and usurious loan sharks; for silver tongued pimps and phony prophets, thieving politicians and vendors of sex and religion, fake healers and fortune tellers and atrocious peddlers of narcotics and death.

HARLEM: Whose expansive bosom is nestling place, hiding place, haven and hell, for the . . . black and brown, tan and yellow children. . . . And no matter how full her house gets she never refuses them a helping hand, never scorns, never complains, is always understanding.

HARLEM: Here slum life is the total sum of life for so many thousands of her children, with only fifty percent of the children under eighteen years old living with both parents; here forty-nine percent of the dwelling units is dilapidated, twenty-five percent is overcrowded; here the average *family* income approximates $3,723, whereas statistics show the average family needs $6,000 just to make ends meet. . . .

HARLEM: A dingy-dirty cluster of roach crawling, rat infested brownstones and tenement flats, interspersed here and there with housing projects, creating a bizarre effect. . . .

HARLEM: A lucrative colony for white retail merchants. . . . Most, if not all, of these merchants live in neighborhoods where black folks can't live.

Although I'm talking about you, dear Harlem, I love you just the same— with your woes and all, ills and all, laughter and all, your troubles and all. For I see in you a profound beauty, manifested by your ceaseless struggles to mold and fashion something good and meaningful out of it all, in spite of it all (Leaks 1963:263–265).

It is in this setting that the children of Harlem learned whom to trust and whom not; it was here that they acquired preferences in food and clothing style, in language use and bodily movement. Here too they came to understand differentiations in male and female behavior. In short, this was their world, and they tried hard to make Harlem School fit into it, despite the seeming efforts by school officials and teachers to make this impossible. I sought to understand the surrounding social milieu in order to effect a confluence of the children's existence and my own. In some simple but meaningful ways I began to learn.

I serviced my car at local gas stations, shopped in local stores, and walked the neighborhood with children on our free time in order to hear what was spoken about and to see who interacted with whom. I frequented the markets along the streets, with their open and enclosed merchandise stands. I found a place where I bought food frequently. The owner came to recognize me on sight after a time. There was a sign constantly posted in the store advertising milk at 19 cents a quart. This was several cents per quart less expensive than milk sales elsewhere, and I stopped at the store often to shop and try to pick up the aspects of local discourse. One day I selected four quarts of milk and handed the clerk a dollar. I was given only 4 cents change when I expected 24 cents in return. I stood silent for a moment, thinking there had been a mistake. But the clerk paid me little mind; he continued on his business ways, rushing the shoppers along (most of whom were black, some Puerto Rican) bluntly and discourteously. Suddenly the proprietor addressed the clerk, who turned out to be his son: "Not to him. With the others all right, but not with him. Give him the right amount." The clerk hurriedly gave me the rest of my change, saying he had made a mistake.

The proprietor had addressed his son in Yiddish, which I understood well. I realized that the clerk had deliberately tried to cheat me and that it must have been common practice to treat most of the customers this way. I turned to the proprietor and, in Yiddish, told him I would call a policeman if such a thing occurred again. I was told it was only a "small" error and that the clerk thought they "were out" of the 19 cents milk. He thus had charged me the "regular" milk price. How many times had the local women, some of whom spoke little English, been taken in by such practices, being overcharged for items they thought were at lower sales prices (Caplovitz 1963)? I wondered also about other neighborhood conditions: slum housing, unemployment among the adults, illness and health. Who, for example, was to blame for the meager housing conditions? At whose hands did deceit and corruption take place in these matters?

> Who would pay $30 a week for two rooms chopped out of a railroad flat, with broken walls, vermin, furniture that belongs in an incinerator, a front door through which rats enter as freely as the swarming children? Who would pay $30 a week, $65 semi-monthly, $130 a month? The City of New York would and does. Why? The landlords know the answer. And the answer makes them inviolate. One of them said, "I run a pigsty for the City of New York. We're partners. See? The city pays me to keep these people off the street and out of everybody's sight, period. They aren't people. They're drunken, filthy, baby-producing pigs, and as soon as they die off, there are more to take their places. Nobody in City Hall . . . knows how these people live, because if they did, they would scream in their sleep. Me? I sleep, because I'm doing everybody a favor. I give the pigs four walls, and the city appreciates it, or, instead of paying me so well, they'd close me down tomorrow, just like they close down bookie joints and hustlers. But they won't, because there's no place else to put the 150 babies I've got urinating in my halls."
>
> Slums are not a new story in New York. As soon as it took shape, the city became a massive slum. But the institutionalized slum, the publicly supported, high-rental slum, the slum that houses only welfare families, the slum that a child cannot forget, not in sleep, not in the ping of heroin, not in Rockland State Hospital, this is the new social-welfare slum (Horwitz 1963:77).

As a teacher you begin to ask yourself about the perceptions children at Harlem School build from this backdrop of experience. Is a child late to school in the morning because he had to wait on line to go to a bathroom that is not in his apartment? Does a girl complete only part of her homework because she helped bathe her smaller brothers and sisters and then had to cook a meal the night before the homework is due? In the morning before school, is it she who helps with the intricate braiding of her sisters' hair and then goes shopping before she comes to school?

Who are the "heroes" in this social setting? How many parents have stayed awake all night with sick children, encouraging their will to live in the face of severe sickness which could not be attended by a doctor because there was not the 10 dollars to pay him for a home visit? How many mothers have learned to make food for two feed a family of six or seven? And how many teachers, who deny the strengths of the children and attribute characteristics of "laziness" and "lack of concern" to parents, could themselves cope with these same problems (Harrington 1963:67)? How many teachers instead sought classroom gimmicks toward persuading the children, when what was required was a few moments of understanding, if not passion? One had to step into the shoes of the child and search with his mind the nature of the world around him (Baldwin 1963a:68–69).

> As he moves forward within his environment, Man takes with him all the positions that he has occupied in the past, and all those that he will occupy in the future. He is everywhere at the same time, a crowd which, in the act of moving forward, yet recapitulates at every instant every step that it has ever taken in the past. For we live in several worlds, each more true than the one within it, and each false in relation to that within which it is itself enveloped. Some of these worlds may be apprehended in action, others exist because we have taken them in our thoughts; but the apparent contradictoriness of their co-existence is resolved by the fact that we are constrained to accord meaning to those worlds which are nearer to us, and to refuse it to those more distant (Levi-Strauss 1961:396).

If the teacher refused meaning to the child's world, however, he was refusing meaning to his own world as well. And in so doing, Harlem School appeared really as a cultural conspiracy against the child; it took fragments of his existence and turned them into myths to provide a rationale for failing to better educate him. Poverty is being poor in its most fundamental sense, but this may take a variety of forms among different groups (Gladwin 1967: 48–75). There are few, if any, behavioral imperatives in being poor, yet the prevailing mythology at Harlem School revised the meaning of poverty into "disadvantage"; it then transformed "disadvantage" in personal terms, implying that children's failure to learn was the result of disadvantages in their cultural experience. Thus, Harlem School suggested that ineffective learning was attributable to deficiencies in children's personal and social lives. This pompous philosophic mode pervades many schools and is an attempt to exonerate the school of its own failures, while allowing it to build a fantasy philosophy about poor children. It seemed equally clear to me that knowing the lives of children in the home was only partially sufficient; if failure began in the home, as alleged, one had to search carefully the home life of teachers as well. How culturally bound was that life? How provincial and ethnocentric?

7 / "Shut those thick lips! Can't you behave like a human being?"

ARLEM SCHOOL, once you realize it is there, dominates the street on which it is located. Its looks are not substantially different from other schools like it and the descriptions given of them.

> A five-story, gray stone building surmounted by a . . . late Victorian mode, . . . its exterior is grimly institutional—though no more so than the sterile facades of its more modern sisters. . . .
> The interior of the school is also uninspiring at first glance. The narrow corridors are dim and deeply scarred and exude the unmistakable odor of that disinfectant that seems to be used in American public schools and nowhere else. . . . Besides being a "K-6" (kindergarten to the sixth grade), it is also a "special service" school, which means it is called upon to perform a whole range of functions over and above those assigned to public elementary schools in other neighborhoods (Schickel 1964:3).

Closer examination reveals an odor from children's having urinated on radiators and an occasional broken window resulting from children's playing ball against the walls after school each day. Through the open windows poured the thick gray-black smoke from tenement stacks adjacent to it. Harlem School is a "neighborhood school," which means that its children are from the immediate locale. More than its physical appearance is conveyed to those who attend school there and to those who work there. Once within its walls, enmeshed in its educational exploits, it becomes a place not easily forgotten. Its children are almost all black with an occasional white Puerto Rican child sometimes present in its classes. It is another school for which statistics of achievement have been collected.

> Harlem may not be absolutely typical of all the city's Negro ghettos, but there is little reason to suppose that its schools are much different from those of others. There are twenty elementary schools and four junior high schools in Central Harlem. On an average, the record of academic achievement in these schools shows a marked inferiority in the attainment of grade level; and what is worse, the children suffer a progressive deterioration with the passage of years. In reading comprehension, for example, from 13.2 to 39.6 per cent of the pupils in third grade are below grade level, while from 10 to 36.7 per cent are above, but by the sixth grade, from 60.4 to 93.5 per cent score below grade level. . . . The figures are much the same for word knowledge and arithmetic (Decter 1964:32).

Few may be acquainted with these statistics, and fewer still might be concerned with them. But for the children who have attended Harlem School only to find that they are unequipped with formal skills for better job employment or the pursuit of further education, it has momentous meaning. For if it is indeed true that "one of the most significant facts about human nature may be that we all begin with the natural equipment to live a thousand kinds of lives and end having lived only one" (Geertz 1966:5–6), the kinds of lives Harlem School children will live are in great measure determined within its walls. The teachers at Harlem School are in more than one sense the keepers of hundreds of lives. Where a person will live, whom he will marry, the kind of job he will hold, the well-being of his children, indeed, where he will be buried, are closely connected with the kind of formal education he receives.

Many of the children, as did Courtney and Kenny in Opportunity Class, deny the relevance of schooling in their lives, perhaps because Harlem School has been irrelevant. Rather than have their will submerged, children rebelled in a variety of ways. Manuel's had been a silent rebellion. Kenny's was more overt. Courtney's tactics were guile and manipulation. These were not strategies brought initially to school by the children, but actions developed there. They were, in a sense, personality survival tactics. They were defensive maneuvers against the attacks of teachers.

Mr. Dorf, for example, punished misbehaving children by putting them in his metal teacher's closet and locking the door. He then banged on the sides creating a deafening noise for the child, who cringed in the darkness. This would deter the child from "talking out without raising his hand."

Other teachers punished children who left their seats "without permission" by making them stand for the remainder of the day. Still others refused to allow children to go to the bathroom, as a punitive measure when they were disobedient, apparently delighting in this "biological warfare." Often children urinated in their clothing, facing embarrassment and ridicule. Another favorite method of disciplining was ear tweaking, a rather painful application of learning.

Directives from the principal's office sometimes encouraged these practices, however inadvertently. We were told, for example, to "check the 'out-of-room' book periodically and compliment children who do not leave the room frequently. (A positive approach is more effective in reducing the number of children leaving the room.) Refer to the nurse those who go to the lavatory excessively."[1]

A barrage of directives was steadily issued by the school administration, usually concerned with regulating children's behavior. Very few directives dealt with more effective ways of handling subject material or suggestions

---

[1] Innumerable guidelines for procedure emanated from the school office. The quotation cited is from "Teacher's Responsibilities." It prescribed procedures for maintaining maximum order in the classroom; n.d.

on how to enhance personal expression, nor did the orders received always make sense. We were given suggestions, as in one instance, on "starting a rhythm band." This informed us how children might be introduced to musical instruments to learn about the orchestra. Yet, in the time I had spent at Harlem School, I had never seen a musical instrument other than a piano.

We were also encouraged to keep an "anecdotal record" on children who were troublesome. Items were to be checked off, such as: "uses bad language," "does not get along with teachers," "unresponsive," "extremely restless," and "bizarre behavior." These records were to "prove the case" against recalcitrant children and would help in having children removed from classes if teachers requested this. A child could thus be proved guilty without benefit of defense, for if the teacher does not speak for the child, who does?

Harlem School was not solely an agency of cultural transmission in an educational sense, but an agency of personality restriction. It did not serve to connect the child and the larger cultural world so that the child would eventually be passed into that world in confidence; it served more to tell the child that he was unacceptable as he was, and that he would have to be substantially changed in order to fit the images others had for him. Children, however, could be expected to object to this characterization of them, and they did. Perhaps it took the form of truancy, or urinating on walls and radiators, carving on desks, dropping blackboard erasers out windows, or "refusing" to learn. Whatever the tactic, it usually had its promptings.

> When you're a kid, everything has some kind of special meaning. I always could find something to do, even if it was doing nothing. But going to school was something else. School stunk. I hated school and all its teachers. I hated the crispy look of the teachers and the draggy-long hours they took out of my life from nine to three-thirty. I dug being outside no matter what kind of weather. Only chumps worked and studied. . . .
> Always it ended up the same way: I got up and went to school. But I didn't always stay there. . . . It was like escaping from some kind of prison (Thomas 1967:64).

The school was not a source of joy and exhilaration for many children, and it may well be true that children fail because "life outside the school is so much more compelling than life inside; that a student is psychologically absent during the hours he spends in class" (Jencks 1966:147). Entanglements are avoided in school; they are reserved for neighborhood friends instead. Few, if any, children would consider Harlem School teachers as friends. Thus, the peer group and close siblings become for most children the primary agents of cultural transmission.

> My brother, Caleb, was seventeen when I was ten. We were very good friends. In fact, he was my best friend and, for a very long time, my only friend.
> I do not mean to say that he was always nice to me. I got on his nerves a lot, and he resented having to take me around with him and be responsible for me when there were so many other things he wanted to be doing. Therefore, his

hand was often up against the side of my head, and my tears caused him to be punished many times. But I knew, somehow, anyway, that when he was being punished for my tears, he was not being punished for anything he had done to me; he was being punished because that was the way we lived; and his punishment, oddly, helped unite us. More oddly still, even as his great hand caused my head to stammer and dropped a flame-colored curtain before my eyes, I understood that he was not striking *me*. His hand leaped out because he could not help it, and I received the blow because I was there. And it happened, sometimes, before I could even catch my breath to howl, that the hand that had struck me grabbed me and held me, and it was difficult to know which of us was weeping. He was striking, striking out, striking out, striking out; the hand asked me to forgive him. I felt his bewilderment through the membrane of my own. I also felt that he was trying to teach me something. And I had, God knows, no other teachers (Baldwin 1967:118, 157).

So much of the children's lives and ways was derived in the community, but was found unacceptable in the school. When some could not find outlet for their feelings in the school, they found themselves more and more attracted to events in the neighborhood.

I used to feel that I belonged on the Harlem Streets and that, regardless of what I did, nobody had any business to take me off the streets. . . .

To me, home was the streets. I suppose there were many people who felt that. . . .

When I was very young—about five years old, maybe younger—I would always be sitting out on the stoop. I remember Mama telling me . . . not to move away from in front of the door. Even when it was time to go up . . . I never wanted to go, because there was so much out there in that street. . . .

I could go out in the street for an afternoon, and I would see so much that, when I came in the house, I'd be talking and talking for what seemed like hours. Dad would say, "Boy, why don't you stop that lyin'? You know you didn't see all that. You know you didn't see nobody do that." But I knew I had (C. Brown 1966:415).

Harlem School was not only antagonistic to many of the children, but dull too; no relationship existed between class and what they had learned in family and neighborhood. Indeed, it was as if the school demanded of children that they relinquish all they knew and assume entirely new postures for themselves. And the reasons for this demand were never fully clear to them. For what purpose were they to be changed? Was it for some future benefit, or to ease the burden of teachers' school lives?

When an anthropologist sees a person learning something in a primitive culture he asks himself, "What is he learning it for?" The answer is usually the obvious one—in order that the person may be able to survive in the culture. Thus, if a boy learns to hunt, it is in order that he may become a hunter and live by hunting; and if he learns gardening, it is to become a primitive farmer and live by farming. There is in such a culture a congruence or complementarity between what a child learns and what he will become. Of course, the whole process of becoming is also clear to a primitive child; for as soon as he is capable of objective knowing, he knows what he will become. . . . We also observe that . . . there is no separation between learning and life.

Once we realize that in our society there is not only a lack of complementarity between what children learn and what they will become, but also that our elementary school . . . tends to conceal rather than to reveal the realities of our culture . . . then we get an idea of why, in many classrooms, the teaching . . . tends to become a problem, even a burden (Henry 1963:35, 36).

There are incongruities, then, in the education of children at Harlem School. They are not always apparent, however, nor are the reasons for their prevalence perceptible to teachers in every instance.

> Perhaps we should be more explicit about the pressures to which the child is subject. The cultural context within which these appear is, of course, that children cannot just be allowed to grow up; they must be wisely directed. . . . What is not made explicit to the child and is probably perceived by only a few . . . teachers is that their own role is dependent upon child accomplishment (Kimball 1963:280).

This fact is extremely important to realize: the failure of children at Harlem School is also the failure of the teachers, just as individual success may be related to teachers' efforts. Culture is a group phenomenon and even individual expressions of it are the result of group influences. If the child slips back in his educational achievement, it is likely that a cultural shove was provided in that direction. Learning not to learn is just as effective as learning to learn.

It was my own view that too much attention was likely paid to the "emotional" condition of children who did not achieve rather than to the social and cultural factors influencing the learning situation. I had realized early in my experience that children have different learning styles. Until now "little careful analysis is given how the child's learning might improve simply by concentrating on the way he works and learns, rather than on his affective reasons for not learning" (Riessman 1964:51). And equal attention has to be paid to the differences in teaching styles. Learning style and teaching style combine through the medium of subject matter—in a specific cultural context—to effect educational transmission.

> The corpus of learning . . . is reciprocal. A culture in its very nature is a set of values, skills, and ways of life that no one member of the society masters. Knowledge in this sense is more like a rope, each strand of which extends no more than a few inches along its length, all being intertwined to give solidity to the whole. The conduct of our educational system has been curiously blind to this interdependent nature of knowledge. We have "teachers" and "pupils," "experts" and "laymen." But the community of learning is somehow overlooked (Bruner 1966:45).

LEARNING NOT TO LEARN

If one examined the average school day at Harlem School he would discover various educational procedures that are found in other schools. Some approaches seemed standard, even immutable. Yet, the implications of these procedures for learning were not as readily perceived. It seemed to me that the very format for the instructional sequence followed each day encouraged children to see subject presentation as tenuous and tentative. The children saw no connecting link among the fragments of material offered them. Rarely was a child permitted to bring his involvement in subject matter to an extensive probing. His passions were not brought to bear in any meaningful engagement in the content of learning. This can be illustrated by drawing out the events on an average school day.

Children flock to school each morning and line up outside the gates. They get to their classrooms shortly thereafter and become incorporated in the routines prescribed for them. Various norms, sometimes unstated, govern their actions. For example, it is not expected, nor permitted, that a child be immediately allowed to go to the bathroom upon arrival in the morning. Similarly school culture prescribes that when a boy has gone to the bathroom during the day, only a girl may go next—as if this were to "preserve democracy" in the classroom. These procedures are not seen as mysteries by teachers or children; they are carried out as "natural" and normal events. Thus, it seems altogether proper that reading and writing lessons predominate as these are seen as requirements for effective later participation in a literate culture.

Customarily the teacher attempts to capture the collective imagination of the children at the outset of each day with a group assignment—penmanship, let us say. While the children practice their letters, they are summoned in groups for reading. The groups may be given names to distinguish reading achievement levels and to help children derive a sense of common membership with others in the group. One teacher at Harlem School named the three reading groups in her class the "Sharks," the "Barracudas," and the "Flounders." These were, of course, allegorical for the "Bright," the "Average," and the "Dull." The children interpreted the meaning of these labels quite easily, just as they had been able to understand the meaning of footprints on the bindings of books. Even the "Dull" knew they were so perceived, and some refused to read as an objection to their designation, often complaining, "We never get any interesting stories to read."

As each group is brought forth, a child may complain that he has not yet finished his penmanship assignment. The teacher, however, insists he join the group. During the reading this same child might not be called upon nor get actively involved over the procedings. It may not be "his turn" to read on this day, leaving him with only a peripheral interest in what is going on. Soon thereafter he and his classmates might be involved in a continuing variety of subject explorations, including arithmetic, social studies, art, science, music, and more. None of those is ever brought to completion, but is postponed until that subject time is rescheduled.

Mixed in with these wanderings may be an unplanned itinerary that would include messages from the school office, a dispute over a pencil, the collection of milk and cookie money, even an occasional fire drill. At other times during a day there are an assembly period, a gym period, recess, and so on. These repeated partial excursions into the nature of subject matter render the child only partially aware and almost wholly uncommitted to that subject matter.

It is as if he is being told that the bits of learning he is presented with are after all only temporary, and that he must be ready to relinquish his accruing insights at any given time in order to go on to other involvements. He learns in this way to "play it cool," knowing that his feeling for his subjects cannot be intense or lasting.

This appraisal may be denied by some, but at Harlem School the proof of it was evident, just as it is evident in the junior and senior high school where the fragmenting of learning is built into a format of brief fifty-minute periods for the various subjects. The constant clanging of bells punctuates the day to reassert this arrangement. In college, continuing this accepted pattern, students and subject material become even more anonymous in oversize classes, where a student's grades often become the only proof of his existence. What made Harlem School a bit more unique was that these practices—and children's subsequent underachievement—were given a mythical rationale. Teachers had a common agreement that "those" children had to be presented with material in short bursts, as it were, because they "couldn't concentrate for long." It occurred to me, however, that the children's concentration was obviously shortened by the very procedures employed in teaching them. A commitment to subject content was not built up, but denied. "Lack of readiness," as it was alleged in behalf of children, was really a lack of readiness among teachers. A child could not extensively pursue a topic to a satisfactory conclusion, perhaps because teachers' own knowledge of the topic was limited. Elementary school teachers are generalists who usually do not have a particular subject specialty for which they have prepared in formal training. They may indeed be jacks-of-all-trades, masters of none.

When such procedures prevail, one's success with children cannot be measured by the children's internalizations of knowledge or their personal investments in content fields, for these do not occur. Instead, children are evaluated and estimated for their worth on a behavioral basis. That is why discipline is so important in the slum school. One can excuse his ignorance of subject matter by translating this ignorance into some alleged dysfunction in children's conduct. I learned soon enough that the administrators at Harlem School would more likely evaluate my own teaching efforts, not by what children learned, but by my bulletin board display, my disciplinary techniques, or the class play we performed in the assembly during the year.

An example of this kind of thinking came at the end of my second year at Harlem School. None of the children in my "average" fifth-grade class read at grade level; some of the children began the year reading at second- and third-grade reading levels. I had worked very hard with two children in particular, Ronald and Charlene, to bring them close to grade level. I felt myself successful with them at the end of the school year, though they had attained only fourth-grade reading level. They had begun the year reading just beyond the primer stage. This represented to me a distinct effort and capability on the part of the two children, and I was confident that they would subsequently reach expected attainment standards. Thus, I was very surprised when Mr. Green told me that Ronald and Charlene would not be promoted. When I asked why this had to be, I was told that it was undesirable to pass children on to the next grade if they were two years behind in reading. I protested that the work of Ronald and Charlene was satisfactory in other subject areas and that they had shown deliberate improvement in reading as well. It would be punishing them, I submitted, for their hard work and effort, and it would be penalizing me for the investment I made in their potential and demonstrated desire to improve. My arguments were fruitless. There was an established pattern at Harlem School: records counted more than feelings. If children were disappointed, one could understand why. They often lost conviction in their own desires and abilities and learned not to try too hard so that they would not be repeatedly denied in their efforts. If you are going to fail, you may as well not try hard to succeed.

In another effort to help Ronald and Charlene I was again overruled. I had learned who the children's teachers would be the next year after placements had already been made. It was customary to do it this way at Harlem School. When children were placed in new classes, it was not with any specific thought in mind that certain teachers can work better with certain children. In this instance I thought that Ronald would do better with Charlene's teacher and that Charlene would fare better with Ronald's assigned teacher. I spoke to the two teachers in question, and they agreed that we should switch the children for the next year. I told Mr. Green of the agreement and formally requested the change. Mr. Green told me it would be "too much trouble" to switch them because rosters had already been made out. When I pleaded on the basis of sound educational principle he told me, "You can switch a boy for a boy, or a girl for a girl, but never a boy for a girl."

I was stunned by this. He saw the children as statistics, not people. His explanation was that too much clerical revision would be necessitated. For example, if there were seventeen boys and fourteen girls in a class, the roster would read "17 + 14." One could switch a girl from another class in place of a girl and the roster would still indicate "17 + 14"; but if a girl were switched for the removal of a boy, the roster would have to read "16 + 15." The administrative upheaval would be too great. This is indeed hard to believe, but this is how the situation ended.

DISCRIMINATION WITH AND WITHOUT PREJUDICE

Many other practices at Harlem School were equally absurd, in the classroom and out. For example, it was generally thought that children who "can't learn" are "good with their hands." It is difficult to find objective evidence for this, yet almost all lessons would culminate by teachers telling children,

"Now draw a picture of what you learned."[2] Crayons were often used as a substitute for more extensive knowledge of subject matter by teachers. They often replaced needed instruction.

"Very poor children need hope in order to achieve. So do those who work with them" (Henry 1965:34). The policies adopted at Harlem School seemed designated to preclude hope for everyone. The incidents with Ronald and Charlene were, at the least, discouraging. They were not perhaps the result of direct prejudice, but of ignorance and too little concern for the feelings of children. They were matters not of the heart, but of routine. There were, however, other practices that were more overt and of even greater impact on the minds of the children.

Miss Matthew's subtle denigration of the children was a case in point. She was the leader of the fifth-grade assembly during my second year at Harlem School. When the children came in each week, she presided at the assembly and read a passage from the Bible during opening exercises. Several teachers noticed that Miss Matthew read the same passage each week. It turned out not that it was a favorite psalm of hers, but that she felt the "dopey kids didn't know the difference, anyhow." She told us that she objected to their "bowing their heads and praying, when they don't know what the hell it's all about." Perhaps she objected to the children sharing the same God with her.

In a similar type of encounter Mr. Hecht once approached me and remarked, "You're an anthropologist; why, when these kids are born so musical, can't they even sing the Star-Spangled Banner correctly?" At first I thought he was kidding, but he pressed the issue. He really believed that black children were innately possessed of a musical quality. When I offered that no one is "born musical," he suggested I was uninformed. Finally I asked Mr. Hecht why he didn't institute a well-developed music program at Harlem School in order to extend and make use of children's "inborn" musical ability, but he walked away, irritated, to join in the singing himself.

To me the most subtle, yet most openly outrageous form of derogation was employed by Mrs. Carp. Her class preceded ours down the stairway at dismissal time each day. Without fail, every afternoon, she turned to her children, halted them and shouted: "Shut those thick lips! Can't you behave like human beings?" Even had Mrs. Carp not realized what she was saying, it was altogether too clear to the children. At other times they were referred to as "wild," "crazy," "animals in a zoo."

Mr. Norman was another teacher who, though capable of being a fine teacher, undermined children at times. Like others after being at Harlem School for many years, he had adopted a variety of denigrating forms of

---

[2] Many teachers consistently employed this procedure, though it is not designed as an art lesson in the formal sense. It was an "escape valve" when one did not know what more to do or if one wanted to "take it easy." I might conjecture that this is why sex education is not taught in the public schools, for then children would have to "draw pictures of what they had learned."

behavior by which he vented his own discontent and frustration on the job. He stood in the hallway when children entered in the afternoon and mockingly addressed them in an assumed southern drawl. Some children simply dismissed his actions, while others gazed in anger at him. Mr. Norman had a favorite routine: he unbefittingly extended his hand to a child and mimicked him by drawling, "Gimme five, man." The child unknowingly smiled and "slapped skin" with Mr. Norman, who then called after the child as he left, "Prehensile lips!"

Perhaps the child at first did not understand the meaning of "prehensile lips," but sooner or later he understood and he did not remember Mr. Norman fondly.

I too realized how a prejudiced remark might even be made without intention when talking to children. Such an instance occurred in class one day. We were periodically required to check children's addresses, just as it was sometimes ordered that we take an ethnic count of children in the class. A teacher was to indicate how many children in the class were Negro or white. One was not supposed to speak to the children about this, but simply to make the appraisal casually. If one were "uncertain," he was to check the category "other" provided for on the form. This was an occasion for great mirth among some teachers, who delighted in categorizing Puerto Rican children as "other." Their hilarity was marked in lunchroom sessions on the days these "ethnic inventories" were made.

I was noting children's addresses on this particular occasion and had almost finished calling on all the children for verification when Marty, who sat just in front of my desk, asked: "Where do you live?" I did not think about my answer and simply repeated an address given by several of the children who lived in the same building. It simply had come to mind because so many of them had stated it. I was merely being lighthearted. However, Marty literally fell from his chair, seemingly hurt. I jumped up to see what was wrong, when I noticed he was doubled up with laughter. It came to me immediately. Marty was laughing so hard because my response had placed me entirely out of cultural context. He, and I, knew that no white people lived on the street I had mentioned. If he ever saw me coming out of one of those old brownstone tenements on that block, it would be the most hilarious sight he had ever seen. My remark was really a mockery of his cultural life. Had it been a deliberate jibe, it would have deserved scorn, not merely laughter. It made me realize how often my own and other teachers' behavior, however innocent, might be interpreted as prejudiced, the fact that Marty found it amusing notwithstanding.

It is little wonder that children reject the school and teachers. In fact it is often necessary to do so in order to maintain an acceptable image of oneself.

> Any Negro born in this country who accepts American education at face value turns into a madman—*has* to. Because the standards that the country pretends to live by are not for him, and he knows that by the time he starts pledging allegiance to the flag. If I had believed, if any Negro on my block had really

believed what the American Republic said about itself, he would have ended up in Bellevue. And those of us who did believe it *did* end up in Bellevue. If you are a Negro, you understand that somehow you have to operate outside the system and beat these people at their own game—which means that your real education essentially occurs outside of books.[3]

It is difficult to tell which actions against children are more objectionable than others; the examples proliferate. Several teachers at Harlem School delighted in threatening to summon a child's parent when they knew definitely that the child was an orphan or his parent was not living in the home. This embarrassed the child and made him feel to blame if he had been adopted or was living with relatives. It would be serious enough if only Harlem School provided the backdrop for such unforgivable treatment of children, but unfortunately such things occur in other schools as well. Mr. Gould spoke of his friends, also teachers, at other schools in Harlem who delighted in destroying the work of children in front of them. Mr. Gould himself referred to the work of children as "rubbish." Most often he did not even look at their assignments, but collected them and threw them in the trash. At other times he ripped work up, dropped it on the floor, and made the children clean it up. It is sad, to be sure, that Mr. Gould has his counterparts.

> If Stephen began to fiddle around during a lesson, the Art Teacher generally would not notice him at first. When she did, both he and the children around him would prepare for trouble. For she would go at his desk with something truly like a vengeance and would shriek at him in a way that carried terror. "Give me that! Your paints are all muddy! You've m⁀de it a mess. Look at what he's done! He's mixed up the colors! I don't know why we waste good paper on this child!" Then: "Garbage! Junk! He gives me garbage and junk! And garbage is one thing I will not have." Now I thought that that garbage and junk was very nearly the only real artwork in the class. I do not know very much about painting, but I know enough to know that the Art Teacher did not know much about it either and that, furthermore, she did not know or care anything at all about the way in which you can destroy a human being. Stephen, in many ways already dying, died a second and third and fourth and final death before her anger (Kozol 1967:3–4).

Why would any teacher behave this way toward children? One must assert that racial prejudice was at the root of much of this behavior. Teachers were themselves victims of the Harlem School social system. Some had long before lost sight of their original motivations for wanting to teach. They had adopted an arsenal of techniques and maneuvers over the years by which to subjugate and pacify children. Perhaps this was easier than developing new techniques of instruction. New teachers learned these restrictive techniques early in their experience. Indeed, the person who rejected these was thought of as an idealist or nonconformist. One need not be consciously committed to a social system in order to behave as if to support it (Kimball and McClellan 1962:219–323). And many teachers denied that it was their intention to be brutal or defamatory with children. They had found that their

---

[3] James Baldwin in "Liberalism and the Negro: A Round-Table Discussion" (1964:32).

preparatory college work was not adequate to equip them for work at Harlem School. They came to see the children as obstacles to smooth educational practice. This is true for teachers in other places too.

> Some Chicago schoolteachers chose to remain in a lower-class school for the lengthy period necessary to reach the top of the list for a very desirable middle-class school. When the opportunity to make the move came, they found they no longer desired to move because they had so adjusted their style of teaching to the problems dealing with lower-class children that they could not contemplate the radical changes necessary to teach middle-class children. They had, for instance, learned to discipline children in ways objectionable to middle-class parents and become accustomed to teaching standards too low for a middle-class school. They had, in short, bet the ease of performance of their job on remaining where they were and in this sense were committed to stay (Becker 1960:37).

While teachers at Harlem School were quick to allege the deficiencies of children, I knew it was the attitude of the individual teacher that needed scrutiny (Zamoff 1966:875). Every person, in the last analysis, must hold himself responsible for his own actions. Besides, that which teachers attributed to children was more often accurate attributions of themselves.

> I have seen teachers in ghetto schools resort to mechanical judgements as a means of protecting themselves from facing their own failures. They see in the environment, the family, the home, the native intelligence of the child, the reasons for the children's failures. It is always thought of that way—"their children's failures"; but in fact it usually is a failure in the classroom, which is as much their responsibility as their pupils. When students fail to respond, it is usually not so much because they can't as because the teacher hasn't offered them something to respond to (Kohl 1967:58).

Unfortunately the more teachers at Harlem School ascribed negative tendencies to the children the more likely these teachers were to base their own teaching on these ascriptions. This precluded an appreciation of any child who was not willing to fit this pattern. But teachers foster such a pattern and then reinforce their perceptions when they bring it about. A whole range of children's possible creative reactions is thus submerged.

> I regret to say that teachers in the United States do not give a place of great importance to either *independence in judgment* or *being courageous*. Independence in judgment and being courageous stands . . . lower than in any of the other six countries for which we have data. In fact, it is far more important to teachers in the United States for their pupils to be courteous than to be courageous. It is also more important that pupils do their work on time, be energetic and industrious, be obedient and popular or well liked among their peers, be receptive to the ideas of others, be versatile, and be willing to accept judgments of authorities than to be courageous. Such a set of values is more likely to produce pupils who are ripe for brainwashing than pupils who can think creatively (Torrance 1963:222).

One must add that such a set of values also produces teachers who cannot think creatively.

> Miss Moyle, an O.P.T. teacher (supplementary teachers who relieve the regular classroom teacher), comes in at 11:00 for social studies. These children

are scheduled to study (the syllabus says they *do* study) math, social studies, science, music, and art, although they can't read. Miss Moyle is very amiable with teachers, recently engaged, salt-and-pepper gray in her hair, and happy.

For a month we had walk-ups and skyscrapers, multiple dwellings, and the subway. "You'd be amazed," Moyle would insist, "how many of the children just don't know what the subway is."

"But Miss Moyle, all the children go to every borough with their families over the week-end, visiting relatives, staying overnight. The little boys sneak on and ride the subway all day Saturday by themselves. They ride all over New York; they go to Coney Island, Forty-second Street, and get themselves home on the subways."

Moyle: "Many of them have simply never seen a subway. Many of these children, dwelling in the world's largest metropolitan area, simply grow up without having learned what 'sub-way' means. We're here to teach them about their cultural environment, such as the subway" (Greene and Ryan 1965:34).

This "innocent" unawareness of teachers is so often turned around and reshaped into an array of myths and distorted allegations about children. Children are seen as "deprived" and "underprivileged," yet it is not always clear what their deprivation or underprivilege is, particularly in relation to classroom performance. Children cannot simply be incapable of learning because inappropriate methods have been employed in teaching them. This cannot be a workable pedagogic position. The belief that they cannot learn is no doubt more potent in fulfilling this suggestion. Perhaps a change in philosophic orientation is needed. In some instances teachers have come to recognize such a necessity.

A breakthrough in my own thinking about formal education at Blackfish Village came about in the metamorphosis of my original research orientations. I had proposed to investigate what it is about village life that makes Indian pupils so refractive to formal education and why Indian pupils fail in school. As I observed and participated in village life and in the classroom, I realized that posing the query in such terms narrowed the perspective of the search. There is another question to ask one which can be considered an alternative but which is, I think, better regarded as a complement to my original orientation: How do schools fail their . . . pupils (Wolcott 1967:131)?

A willingness to explore alternatives in facilitating children's learning brings also an immense hope. In so doing, it may be that we discover ways of teaching all children, not only the poor and discriminated against. Certainly this would be better than the present estrangement children and teachers feel in our schools, particularly where ethnic minority children attend. It would allow the development of new theories of instruction, so glaringly missing at the present time (Bruner 1963). A comparative view of education in other settings is also relevant.

If there is anything written clear across the almost infinite diversity of primitive society, it is that the group molds its members toward emotion, toward the experience of crises of realization and of conscience, and toward a profoundly romantic world-view which includes a profoundly romantic view of man in the world. . . . Hence, to an extent hardly imaginable in our modern society and state, the ultimate concentration of the primitive group is upon education—upon personality development. Every experience is used to that end, every specialized skill and expression is bent to that end. There results an integration of body-mind and of individual-group which is not automatic, not at the level of conformity ad habit, but spontaneous . . . and at the level of freedom. Many readers will resist this statement, and as in most matters that are essential in human life, the proof that it is true cannot be coercive. Modern man does not like any suggestion that he has fallen away from a greater good which he once had. But let once the mind be opened, let once a curious and sympathetic interest be born, and then the data of ethnology yields overwhelming conviction on the statement here made (Collier 1947:22–23).

As I continued to look at what was happening at Harlem School, I came to think that it may be possible that a social system can survive and perpetuate itself even though it does not serve to support its individual members. It may likewise be that individuals can behave in ways that offer no substantial psychological supports for that behavior. Filling immediate need does not necessarily bring subsequent satisfaction with it. Teachers at Harlem School might have sought expedient means to meet immediate need to reduce frustration in the classroom, but they could not be happy with the long-range results. They repeatedly expressed ambivalence and annoyance about themselves, and continually they had to force their own reassessment of their role with the children. The children too asked a reassessment.

> How would you have us, as we are?
> Or sinking neath the load we bear?
> Our eyes fixed forward on a star,
> Or gazing empty at despair?
>
> Rising or falling? Men or things?
> With dragging pace or footsteps fleet?
> Strong, willing sinews in your wings,
> Or tightening chains about your feet?
> (Johnson n.d.)

8 / White lies about black children

IN PREPARING for my third year at Harlem, I knew I would have to overcome all the subtle and open prejudgments prevalent there. In fact, I knew that the many prejudices harbored by teachers were the result of an accrual of myths about the children, so that these became normally acceptable credos. It was a gradual and cumulative process by which teachers were infused with these notions. When I first came to Harlem School, I was apprised that the children were slow learners, had low IQ's and were not interested in learning. Most of the children, I was told, were of poor families—many on welfare—and had parents who were too busy or unconcerned about school affairs. Before long I became aware of a rather large inventory of myths about the children. If one myth no longer seemed to hold at times, it was conveniently replaced by a new one. When these were disputed, the children were simply labeled as "disadvantaged." This was to leave the alleged incapacities of children to anyone's imagination. It was the final word in a repertoire of jargon. In fact, it was clear that the school itself was a chief myth-monger, contributing many of its misconceptions about children to the larger public. It also was evident that the existence of these falsehoods was derived from, and lent testimony to, the dysfunctional character of Harlem School.

> Urban educators are isolated from the cultural and social milieux of their pupils. . . . Knowing little of their pupils' life, and terrified and appalled by what they do discover, they justify their avoidance with a "vacuum ideology" of cultural deficiency and deprivation which ignores and derogates the values and knowledge that pupils have acquired in their homes and neighborhoods. Meanwhile, the educators preach morals and manners that are vacuous or fatuous given the realities of the domestic lives of the children (Wax, *et al.* 1964: 114).

Those who accepted these attitudes at face value were as much the victims of an unsupportable ideology as were the children. It was really another technique to add to the pedagogic kit possessed by teachers. It was another classroom routine. One might also imagine that it was part of a teacher's training in educational methods courses. For example, a college instructor might inform teacher trainees on how to teach reading, describing the various methods and techniques in so doing. Then he might add that if none of these works, invoke the method of seeing the child as disadvantaged, a technique which will mitigate the failure of all those previously tried approaches. Though this may sound unfair to some, it is important to enunciate this pattern because point of view among teachers is similar to classroom use of material. But it does more; it transforms children to fit that point of view.

> Children everywhere have been trained to fit culture as it exists; and to the end that they should not fail to fit, man has used the great ingenuity of which he is capable. As a device for teaching what was necessary and preventing deviation, education became an instrument of narrowing the perceptual sphere, thus defining the condition of being absurd; of learning to be stupid; of learning to alienate one's Self from inner promptings.
>
> Turning to the contemporary school we see it as a place where children are drilled in cultural orientations, and where subject matter becomes to a very considerable extent the instrument for instilling them. This comes about, however, not only because school, as the heartbeat of the culture, naturally embodies and expresses the central preoccupations, but also because schools deal with masses of children, and can manage therefore only by reducing them all to a common definition (Henry 1963a:320–321).

The common denominator of "disadvantage" which was applied to children at Harlem School, however, denied some fundamental assumptions about what we know of the human individual. Certainly no person remains the same over time. Personality formation and expression function in a temporal context, but at Harlem School all were regarded as alike from kindergarten to sixth grade. The fact that a child was judged as incapable and singled out for special classes because of some "disadvantage" was an even greater disadvantage to the child. He essentially was prevented from eradicating the false image others had of him. Even if a child's classroom performance was hindered by outside experience, the school's posture did not allow an attempt to alter the cause of the child's disadvantage, but reflected only on its results. It served not as an agency of change, but for continuation of the conditions it decried.

I felt I had to seek the contrary evidence for the many negative assertions about children. I wondered, for example, why some children did succeed. If all of them were "disadvantaged," none should succeed. It was soon apparent that none of the assertions stood the test of empirical examination. Teachers had only emotional and intuitive support for their views. In almost every instance they merely believed things to be as they saw them, with no significant proof.

The most common and prevalent assertion was that the child had an inability to "postpone immediate gratification for future reward." This implied that he could not see long-range, more important goals. More than this, it suggested that he could not work steadily and consistently at his studies. Of course at the root of this were the child's family and other neighborhood conditions, it was said. One teacher even offered that the reason black athletes excelled in short distance races was because they too had the inability to postpone immediate gratification for future reward—that is, they

would not enter the mile, for example, because it took too long to determine the winner. By contrast, the argument went, Jews were alleged to have
the perseverance to see long-range goals because they had historically been
expelled from Egypt, Spain, Germany, and other places, thereby being infused with a capacity to wait for better times in the future. One teacher
even argued that the creation of Israel was an example of this capacity
among Jews.

Some may feel that this absurd argument could not have been offered,
but a look at Harlem School would reveal the existence of this myth in a
variety of forms. How easily disproved it is. Offering even some minimal
data about poor people refutes the argument. Of all the people in our midst
who learn to be patient and wait (for almost everything other people always
have on hand), it is the poor. They wait for welfare checks, for overdue
repairs to their homes, for job openings, and for improved social conditions
which they hope will bring better and equal opportunity. The poor are those
who attend medical clinics when they are sick, not having a doctor always
on call for every emergency and frequently being without the money to pay
for one. It is, one must say, more than insulting to declare that the inability
to postpone gratification is a characteristic of the poor. Postponement of
gratification typifies so many aspects of their lives.

I must agree that "cultural differences have been rather overplayed in
discussions of the disadvantaged. Idiosyncracies of culture are of more interest
to the tourist than to the advocate of progress and change. What is most
significant about the culture of the disadvantaged is that its essentials are
much like those of the advantaged, minus the material comforts . . . that
are their by-products" (Sexton 1965:9–10). If anyone at Harlem School was
unable to postpone immediate gratification for future reward, it was the
teacher, the person who was unwilling to try and try again to stimulate the
child by new teaching procedures. "Perhaps it is not the disadvantaged who
have capitulated to their environment, but the teachers who have capitulated
to theirs" (Riessman 1962:23).

If some of the myths had been true, they did not serve as spurs to further
insight or the enhancement of learning. Teachers did not act positively on
these myths, in any case. Innovation in the classroom was not the goal. What
did result was a "deeducation" of the child and the fact that a child in
poverty without a successful formal education is more likely to be poor in
adulthood as well.[1] Thus, the children of the children now in school would
have to be saddled with the same inexcusable rationale for attaining a meager
education when they got to school—because their failures too would be
blamed on family and neighborhood "disadvantage."

Another myth elaborated at Harlem School was that the child was "nonverbal." This suggested that he had an inferior inventory of words and was

---

[1] See Clark (1965), particularly the section on "Ghetto Schools: Separate and Unequal," pp.
111–153.

frequently without the relevant thoughts for more efficient idea expression. If this deficiency existed, it was thought, it was no wonder that the child did not learn to read and write well. If language and thought are so intimately related, the child was seen as thinking "differently"; thus, no matter the efforts of teachers, a child who is "different" could not be taught like other children. This intimation is particularly sad because it focuses on *how* children think, rather than on *what* they think about. Moreover, it neglects the fact that the difficulty teachers face in communicating with children is considerably related to how teachers talk. Would the child be justified in concluding that the teacher's use of language is deficient and that she is nonverbal because she does not make herself understood by him?

Communication takes place in a social and cultural context; there are rules of the game, so to speak, in conveying a message. The informal aspect of language interaction is sometimes the key to the formal message itself (Hall 1964:154–163). Similarly language is really the medium by which cultural transactions take place, and the anticipations people have of others' intentions are central to communicative success (Hall 1959:118–119). One has to keep in mind the influence of the physical surroundings and the cultural antecedents involved in making the immediate moment seem as it appears (Hall 1960:5–12). If children are made to feel that they have nothing important to say, it is likely that they may say things of no importance, or not say much at all. People need someone to talk to in order to feel like talking. This hardly means that they are nonverbal. To the contrary, the constant complaint of teachers at Harlem School was that the children were always "sounding," talking when "they were not supposed to." The claim that children were nonverbal was really the implicit desire that children should be quiet. The teacher who could keep her children quiet and immobilized was thought by school officials to have a firm and controlling hand with them. For some reason this is a priority that schools maintain, as if quiet education is the best education.

Some teachers pointed to the low reading scores of children as affirmation of the children's verbal inabilities. This was also stretching an already weak point. Children who did not read well might have read better, had the reading material been more in keeping with their experiences and interests. There must be a purpose to reading as in other things people do. "You discover that people, when they have any reasons to do it at all, find that literacy is really one of the simplest techniques, compared, for example, to weaving or the variety of skills that people must teach one another. . . . There may be something involved in our own school system that inhibits some people from being able to get a decent start" (Tax 1965:209). There were children in my classes who knew how to iron and fold shirts—a skill many adult females have not mastered—and to cook whole meals because it was meaningful for them to do so. These were not skills valued by the school but neither were the school's values always held dear by the children.

Another claim by school officials was that children were "lazy" and "unclean." They indicated that children had no concern for their appearance and that parents were lax in caring for them. This assertion has often been seen as peculiar and paradoxical, for it is well known that the same parents referred to so frequently find employment as cleaning women and domestics in the homes of those who make such assertions. Indeed, at Harlem School the custodial staff and the cafeteria staff (those who swept and polished the school floors) were often parents of the children at the school. Furthermore, the children accused in this manner were able to maintain their clothing and personal selves in remarkably good style, especially considering the poverty many of them had to live with. Often they had to wear the same apparel day after day, and they made it do because they had to. They were not encouraged to see a distinction between "school clothing" and "play clothing" because it was not financially possible for them. Just a look at the children should have been enough to confirm the real care with which they were treated by parents. Girls, for example, often had a unique and involved network of braids in their hair which must have required long periods of time to arrange properly.

To accuse children at Harlem School of being lazy and unclean seemed to me like accusing an African Bushman of getting his hands dirty after killing and dismembering a kudu, or suggesting that an Eskimo keep the fat and blood stains from his parka after a seal hunt (with a spot cleaner perhaps). Even an attempt by an Eskimo to do so would fail because the drippings would freeze before stains could be prevented. The analogy is not farfetched; it was, in fact, impossible for some of the children to wear the same clothing for long periods of time and keep them looking eternally new. The negative description of children's deportment is more a reflection of inverted school priorities than the failings of children. Schools are very much concerned with propriety and etiquette—children must excuse their absences, raise their hands each time they speak, be quiet on fire drills, and remove the dirt from under fingernails. However desirable some of these "imperatives" might be to some teachers, it must be admitted that they have almost nothing to do with how learning proceeds. I can think of no relationship of cleanliness to learning theory.

One teacher, Mrs. Hoffman, said that the frequent illnesses and absences of the children was a further indication of their failure to take care of themselves: not dressing properly and not being clean. She cited the frequent instances of "asthma" among the children. However, she never referred to the squalid conditions in which children were made to live by the larger society, nor to the run-down conditions of the landlord-neglected tenements, nor to the fact that poor people do not receive the same quality of medical care as do the more well-to-do. For instance, members of minority groups are often underattended in hospitals and clinics. Some at Harlem School suggested that black athletes do not get hurt as often, or as severely, as white athletes. They pointed to the punishment black boxers take so frequently. Sometimes this myth was translated to the emotional state of non-whites. Black children's feelings, they alleged, do not get hurt as easily. This was a ready rationale for neglecting the political and legal rights of poor people as well (Goldberg 1964:57–60). In medical instances, particularly in "inter-racial situations, there is a marked tendency to examine only cursorily those anatomical features of a patient of another race which are characteristic of that race and are (unconsciously, because of prejudice) viewed as tokens of 'inferiority' " (Devereaux 1961:7). A person who is black, being treated by a white doctor, may find that the doctor does not probe extensively enough to determine the root of illness because the doctor may feel that the patient thinks that undue attention is being paid to "wide nostrils" or "thick lips." Irrespective of the intentions, the result is a disservice to the person.

Harlem School also accepted the myth that the child could not learn because "his father was absent from the home." This implied that the child did not get adequate encouragement at home to study and prepare if his father was not in the home. Even where fathers were not present for some reason this claim was tenuous at best. Many middle-class children have fathers at home who pay no attention to their children's schoolwork. Their presence may have nothing to do with children's school achievement. Moreover, the teachers who feel children are handicapped by absent fathers need only pretend that the fathers are present if this belief would improve their methods of working with the children. Children, therefore, would achieve by the "imagined" presence of their absent fathers. This mythical syndrome is similar to the one where teachers assert that a child should have a phonograph at home, a set of encyclopedia, and a separate room for study; yet none of these was present at Harlem School, for the most part. Indeed, in no school is a child given a separate room for isolated study. Is this why they fail? Besides, and even more important, it is outrageous to offer that having a room or a phonograph is prerequisite to a child's right to the best possible education that can be afforded him in the school. A father to help one with his homework is not such a prerequisite either.

Furthermore, mothers are quite capable of encouraging children to want to learn at Harlem School. Most elementary teachers, after all, are women. Should they be replaced in each case by men? Most PTA's are made up of women, too. Mothers at Harlem School waited for their children after school and regularly checked the assignments my children had, despite the many tasks they had to perform without additional assistance. It is easy for white teachers to look at the existence of black children from biased eyes, neglecting that poor people so often have alternative arrangements for martialing social support (Lewis 1966*b*:18–23). There are "accommodations Negroes have worked out in dealing with fatherless families. Grandmothers very often look after the kids. The mother works or goes on relief. The kids identify with stepfathers, uncles, even the mother's boyfriends. How children grow up is a cultural, not a statistical pattern."[2]

The "absent father" myth was contradicted by the teachers themselves

---

[2] See Moynihan (1967), citing Ralph Ellison, p. 17.

so often; that is, they asserted that children's parents were antagonistic to teachers' efforts and even passively encouraged children not to obey and respond in school. If this be the case, then teachers ought to feel that an absent father would be a positive factor in getting children to learn because it removes an "obstacle" teachers claimed existed. One obviously cannot have it both ways. Teachers learned to pick the myth that suited them best at a particular time. Learning procedures have to be examined in the context of the classroom, not in the context of the living room or the bedroom (Landes 1965).

Another negative attribute alleged against the children at Harlem School was that they were of "low intelligence." People pointed to low IQ scores as evidence of this. Intelligence, however, was not measured by children's insights or the activities they engaged in, but by test scores. Teachers, thereafter, assigned behavioral characteristics to the IQ scores. Thus, if a child were a "discipline problem," he was thought to be of low intelligence. Many of the children were, nevertheless, of high intelligence, of great creative potential, and of wide temperamental styles. Ironically some of the same negative characteristics by which they were described were indications of this creativity (Torrance 1962:66–67).

Many children would have achieved higher IQ scores if they had viewed the testing situation as important. Some did not try particularly hard on these tests. Others were puzzled by the language employed, when with another use of language on the examination the children would easily have evidenced the mental processes called for (Havighurst and Neugarten 1957: 228–230). The claim that black and Puerto Rican children are handicapped in intelligence by their "disadvantage" is a modern, and convenient, substitute for long-disproved theories of racial inferiority. Sometimes a "wrong" answer on an intelligence test is actually a better answer, but it reduces the child's score. For example, an intelligence tester posed this problem for a "poor white" child in Kentucky: " 'If you had 10 cows to pasture for your father and 6 of them strayed away, how many would you have left to drive home?' The boy replied, 'We don't have 10 cows, but if we did and I lost 6, I wouldn't dare go home' " (Montagu 1964:82).

One might more appropriately argue that teachers' beliefs about children's innate low intelligence is more an indication of teachers' "lack of intelligence" than of dullness in children. Quite clearly, intelligence test scoring is a matter of children's preparation for, and the relevance of, the tests themselves. "Here again we have evidence in favour of the view that when environments are similar, the test results appear to be similar as well" (Klineberg 1958:17). Teachers who are unfamiliar with the social lives of children at Harlem School find it difficult to perceive the mental ability children must bring to bear in meeting the demands of their existence. Unfortunately "the judgment of the mental status of a people is generally guided by the difference between its social status and our own, and the greater the difference . . . the harsher our judgment" (Boas 1965:21). Children's seeming lack of intelligence at Harlem School may be the result of their unwillingness to conform to the demands of intelligence testing; for them this may well be an intelligent way of denying the school's "technological" description of them.

I was aware of the tendency at Harlem School to explain children's behavior in psychological terms exclusively, rather than in cultural terms. Perhaps "psychology has not yet settled down to the problem of transforming matters of fact—whose acquisition current learning theories explain fairly well—into autonomous matters of importance—which they do not explain at all" (Allport 1961:217). Perhaps too this is why a colleague at Harlem School referred to this kind of thinking as a "sphincter psychology." I do not mean to say that psychology has nothing to contribute in understanding the learning process in slum schools. I do mean to say that many misconceptions about children have been promulgated in the name of psychology. It may be well to look to some alternative points of view.

> Studies of the psychological aspects of child development have been helpful, but much of our energy has been directed toward accumulating those static data which tests and measurements render. This is not the stuff which reveals to us the intricate interdependencies between individual and environment. They do not lend themselves to a statement of the processes which explain growth and change. Furthermore, those who are wedded to their use are trapped in an intellectual procedure which seeks orderliness through the categorization of the atomistic bits and pieces which they have gathered. There is the temptation to label the results obtained as nonsense since the reality they portray is not that of the world they examine but of the operations which they represent (Kimball 1965:161–162).

There is the need then to seek cultural underpinnings for children's behavior and

> . . . to assume optimistically that there is some positive reason for the behavior of any person or any community. Thus, nothing is to be treated negatively. We do not say that groups lack something or they would not do this; rather we recognize limitations on our own understanding of why each group acts in a particular way. But we know the group must have a reason for doing it in its way and try to discover the reason (Tax 1965:209–210).

Still another myth about the children was that "they were unwilling to change" and "were of little worth as they were." This attitude is partly in keeping with the dominant American value that one must strive to better himself constantly; one cannot stand still, so to speak. Status is to be achieved by continual efforts to improve (Lynd 1964:54–113). Pedagogically this implied that the child could not be worked with as he was; he was not sufficiently ready for learning. Thus, if the teacher failed, it was because the child offered insufficient material with which to work. However, the greater the push to alter who children were, the greater was their resistance to change. All persons come to think that they have acquired coherent cognitive systems by which to see the world, and they resist any denial of this by others (Wax 1963:695). What was needed was not a defamation of who the children were, but an affirmation that each child can build and expand his own personality as he acquires knowledge.

Most of us agree that for a teacher to deny a child understanding and affection is to deny him an education. Without these elements of response, the slum child will reject school. . . . Nonetheless, some of us persist in maintaining higher priority for concerns of how teaching proceeds than of how learning occurs. . . . Certainly something more than increased time and organization is needed to effectively instruct those who appear disinterested, their fellows who are belligerent, others who are slow and the remaining host of differing personalities in each classroom. What is required is a greater knowledge of learners and the learning process, more appropriate diagnostic measures to determine scholastic weakness, and methods of teaching that are in conjunction with each pupil's most efficient learning style and pace of accommodation. In short, what is called for is the highest form of respect: understanding (Strom 1965:71).

Understanding is precluded when myth and not reality regulates the lives of teachers in their dealings with children, particularly when those myths are not shared by the persons being described by them. It is sometimes necessary to draw back and to examine one's behavior to see if it does not seem peculiar to others. That which we take for granted, as normal and natural, may seem to us as somewhat unusual when we examine its meaning unemotionally (Miner 1956:503–507). America is an amalgam of many cultural traditions and the contributions of many peoples (Linton 1936:326–327), and the school ought to be one place where these historic and cultural antecedents to our present existence should be appreciated and clarified. Denying the child's worth is a denial of America's most unique potential contribution to human life: the advocacy of cultural pluralism and behavioral diversity.

A further charge against the child at Harlem School was that he "was not interested in education." He was said to be interested in "earthy" things, such as food, sex, or having fun. This is another extraordinary form of ethnocentrism, which attacks the morality of others; in this case, children are the victims. Teachers talked about the Cadillacs in the streets while children were "without food." It was meant to indicate that poor people waste their money, otherwise they would not be poor. This was similar to the argument that parents "would rather be on welfare than get a job." To me the "welfare argument" was as if to say that a person would deliberately break his leg because he knew he could get free medical treatment at a clinic.

The "mowed lawn" argument is another myth in this category. Mr. Gould said that he did not want a black man living next door to him because "he would not keep his property up, and real estate values would go down." Mr. Gould said that he "was not prejudiced, just practical." In talking to Mr. Gould, however, one easily realized that he was more fearful of the prospects that a black man would mow his lawn and maintain his property, for then Mr. Gould would have to seek another reason for attempting to exclude such a person from his neighborhood. It was better, therefore, to keep "undesirable" people from moving into the neighborhood in the first place, lest they turn out to be worthy and substantial persons.

The lack of interest in education ascribed to children is better seen as a lack of motivation and opportunity in education. In addition, one has to be aware of the circumstances in which people live. How might they react were conditions different?

> The social conditions which perpetuate their poverty . . . must be remedied before anyone can judge what kinds of citizens they might be in other, more favorable circumstances. To be able to live a decent life and be respected for it, without being subjected to a blanket damnation that one's personal life cannot remove, is a human right, the granting of which would have immense social repercussions (Benedict 1959:154).

In order to interest the learner, education must first be of interest. It was surprising to me that not more children at Harlem School were disinterested in the education offered them. Apparently many parents prodded their children to learn the ways of the dominant culture in which they would later have to live, so they would be better able to cope with the discrimination and uncertain opportunities they would have to face.

> We were interested to come upon a finding which indicated that members of underprivileged groups had a rather surprising view about the importance of education. Interviewees were asked the question, "What do you miss most in life that you would like your children to have?" Over 50 per cent of the white lower socio-economic group (and 70 per cent of the Negro group) said "education." Even more significant is the fact that the respondents supplied the word "education"; they did not select it from a list of possible choices provided by the interviewer. This would seem to mean that education, at some level, not only is important to this group, but also is in the forefront of their minds (Riessman 1962:10).

It must be made clear at this point that many of the myths about the children come not from their conditions of existence, but from the narrow and confining aspects of school life as these weigh on the teachers. The system itself spells failure and discontent.

> The tradition of success is almost gone—in increasing numbers, teachers and principals live with the expectation of failure and weave a net of excuses. . . .
> All change is resisted because it implies a criticism of the present—and feared, because it will be made without consulting the teachers who will have to live with the results. The hope for leadership has been disappointed so often that people have turned in upon themselves, learned to live with meaningless and fantastically detailed rule books, lost any sense of the possibilities outside the narrow structure of the hierarchy of jobs (Mayer 1965:34).

Unaccepting of the realities of this existence, many teachers find a need to erect make-believe pictures of the children for their own minds. They attribute all ills to a "culture of poverty" in which the children are thought to live. The child is seen as alienated from the school and the larger society, but it is the culture of the school which alienates both teacher and child. Teachers feel the problems of conscience are excused and diffused by claiming a "culture of poverty" for the child. As in the other instances this ideology maintains that one can try to work with the children, but their "culture" provides a barrier to classroom achievement. Never, however, is the "culture of poverty" theme articulated in positive terms; the children's strengths are not enunciated. Yet, if cultures are blueprints for existence—mental maps which the individual carries with him through life—they must enable the person to satisfactorily meet the demands of his existence; they have an adaptive function.[3] Many of the traits which teachers in Harlem School saw as negative in children were positive forms of adaptation to the physical and social environment. In fact, this is a point that must be made: the rejection of school by the children who withdrew or acted out was, for them, a positive response. It served as a safeguard for personal perceptions of self and helped diminish anxiety and loneliness in the school. Their reactions could only be seen as negative when the stimuli for learning might be altered, so that other, more acceptable responses would be sought from the children, making the old reactions no longer relevant. But school policy rarely altered.

If the child is, indeed, seen as "different" at Harlem School and if this difference is supposed to mark him as possessing unbecoming traits, it is in the main the result of the continuing negative portrayal of black people in our culture. Our literature and mass media systems certainly share a major part of the blame for this.

Of critical importance, and of severe implication, is the fact that many children at one time or another come to believe some of these myths about themselves. The school rarely shows black people in advantaged or admired positions. At Harlem School one week in February was set aside for "Negro History Week." It was as if blacks were relevant in American history only in February. Indeed, this was a mockery of what history is really all about. In class, children were not so much the victims of a "culture of poverty" as they were the victims of social differentiation and exclusion. Even the subject matter which was presented to them was distorted. Their legitimate claims on the school and the culture were differentially fulfilled. They saw the school as the institutionalization of inequality.

In any event, the "culture of poverty" is to be seen as taking different forms in different subcultures and within the same subculture. It is also to be seen as different from objective poverty which is so widespread in Harlem. Unfortunately many teachers interpreted the "culture of poverty" as a poverty of culture, an absence of some essential human qualities. Of course no group is devoid of culture, and to suggest it is to imply a "white man's burden" image which children and parents reject. This philosophic form of "colonialism" is to be guarded against (Coles 1965:7, 54–56, 58). And the difference between poverty and a "culture of poverty" must be understood.[4]

When one suggested to school officials that materials presenting more positive and accurate images of blacks and Puerto Ricans be used, he was told that the curriculum did not call for these. In fact, still another myth was put forth. This stated that black peoples "have contributed little, if

---

[3] See Lewis (1965:xlvii). The author relates the many adaptations people in poverty make to their existence by which they learn to maintain a sense of cohesion in their lives.

[4] See Lewis (1966a:19–25). The author gives a brief and clear description of the "culture of poverty" concept.

anything, of significance to history." Blacks, moreover, were described as "childlike" and "having an insignificant past." This, of course, denies what we know of human cultural and biological history and evolution. All people, present and past, have made suitable adaptations to their environments, and all people share the unique human capacity for the development of culture. Anthropologists have long argued and shown that cultures are not comparable in terms of being better or worse than other cultures. The vast range of expression recognized under the term *human nature* has always been varied and part of any people's capability. "In men's observations of one another, there is little to lead them to concentrate on recurring regularity or to induce notions of fixity or law. Everyone develops, with the very experience of living, his own practical skills of interpreting and dealing with other human beings, as a practical necessity" (Kroeber 1966:159). With different experiences and opportunities every man would be yet a different man. The contribution of peoples must be seen in historical perspective. No group is or has been superior to another by innate characteristics.

> In the last 400 years European whites have been in the ascendancy in technical and political developments, in progress achieved through the industrial revolution and in expansion into other parts of the world. However, before this time the torch of civilization had been carried by one dark-skinned group of people after another.
> The Egyptians, the Sumerians (of present-day Iraq), the Hindus, the Chinese, and the Arabs developed mighty civilizations and contributed significantly to the base on which the industrial revolution of Europe was built. There is a long roster of inventions and innovations derived from these peoples that we use today. Some of the more important ones are: the domestication of animals and plants; the wheel; the smelting of bronze, iron and steel; the solar calendar; the zero and a place numeral system; irrigation systems; gunpowder; writing systems; and the printing press (Arensberg and Niehoff 1964:21).

The fact that peoples throughout history have been able to utilize the creations of others for their own purposes is ample testimony that peoples are capable of similar responses in similar circumstances. Despite differences among peoples, real and imagined, all human groups have more in common than in differentiation (Murdock 1945:123–142). To say that the Harlem child is of a group that has contributed little to history is, first, to claim for him membership in a group that is the creation of the describer and, second, to distort the true meaning of being human. Obviously every child is a member of the whole human group before he is anything else. At Harlem School, as in other schools, there was a tendency to exalt the technological and the tangible in human life, rather than the social and the psychological. We tend to think that if a person is better off than another he is indeed a better person. Poor children have had to suffer this interpretation for a long time. Similarly there was the disposition to begin the teaching of history with the coming of Columbus; thus, the black man was viewed only as a slave. Historic derivations and cultural antecedents were not dealt with, nor were the myriad cultures existing in Africa discussed. In fact a turnaround was made by teachers. Because many people in Harlem lived in

poverty, it was asserted that blacks in the past must have endured a similar fate. This attitude also denied and discounted the struggles black people have made in this country and elsewhere for personal and group freedom (Aptheker 1951). One can only conclude that teachers' ignorance of black life in America and in the past was, itself, the result of an inferior education —their own. After all, teachers are the product of our public schools too.

There were, to be sure, many more myths about children at Harlem School, all easily exploded by the available cultural and scientific evidence. Their disproof did not, however, mitigate the shame and pain caused children. Their real disadvantage was their helplessness in combating a system that so denigrated them.

> And unfair is the best that can be said about the situation confronting the Negro child in the segregated classroom. Every experience he has seems calculated to demonstrate to him that he is inferior and should resign himself to be so. The system singles him out, separating him by color from the best schools and the best teachers. The least is demanded of him and expected from him. The prescribed neighborhood he lives in, and the restrictions that shackle the adults he lives with, strongly suggest that his is a lost cause. His life at school combines with the rest of his life to make him see himself as a second-class citizen (Howe 1966:24).

How many pretensions teachers held about the children was difficult to tell at Harlem School. It was said that the child was "more prejudiced against 'his own kind' than others were against him," and that he was "content to live in poverty," as if people prefer poverty to plenty when there is a choice. It was also said that the child "was used to failure, and one should not feel bad about it." No matter the myth, however, one thing was clear: the child's failure was unmistakably the failure of the teacher. No myth could gainsay that.

> They are the slaves who fear to speak
> For the fallen and the weak. . . .
> They are the slaves who dare not be
> In the right with two or three.
> (Lowell 1956:105)

9 / Project class

IN MY THIRD YEAR at Harlem School an opportunity presented itself by which I could attempt to put into practice several of the thoughts I had developed over the previous two years. Mr. Green told me about a special program at the school, then in its third year, involving two classes. It was an attempt to take a more total approach to the education of the children and to bring them a variety of experiences not normally available to them. Students' aspiration levels were to be raised through a special "enrichment" program. Health and social welfare services, club activities, added classroom specialists, extensive trips, and a Saturday school program were to be part of this new approach. Two classes had been chosen for the experiment two years before (when I had first come to Harlem School) when the children were in the third grade. They were now entering fifth grade. Part of the original idea was to keep the children together in each of the classes for the entire four years from third grade through the sixth grade. The brightest class on the third grade had been chosen, along with an "average" class on the grade. The average class had been chosen as a "control group"; officials wanted to make sure that the additional services to be offered the children could be properly evaluated for their influence. If only the bright class had been involved, it would not be easy to ascertain whether their achievement was the result of the services rendered or the usual result of children's normal efforts. Thus, if the academic progress of the average class improved significantly, one might assume that the added services brought to them were responsible for their gains.

Another premise underlying the program was that by keeping children together with the same teacher over an extended period of time one would expect them to build a stronger and more permanent relationship to one another and to the teacher. I asked Mr. Green why then he had spoken to me about joining the program. In fact, I had been asked to become the teacher of the "average class," then known as 5-4. He told me that the bright class, 5-1, had progressed well, but that 5-4 had become an exceedingly difficult problem for the original teacher to handle. There was a wide spread in the children's abilities and the group had become a bad discipline problem. Their teacher had requested reassignment. It was thought that I could "handle" them well.

I thought about the opportunity and then concluded that it would be challenging. Many colleagues, however, told me that I was a fool and a "sucker" for accepting the position. They told me I was the lamb being led to the slaughter. I would regret my decision, they told me. The children were reported to be so unruly that it would be an insurmountable task to teach them. All this notwithstanding, I was anxious to get involved, especially since it was my view that the teacher of class 5-1 was one of the best at Harlem School. Perhaps we would have a chance to work together. I also thought that with an extended effort one might be able to prove that poor children could, indeed, learn if they were given opportunity and understanding. I met with school officials and the children's parents before clásses were to start. I learned as well that Neighborhood Services,[1] a social welfare agency that had many dedicated members on its staff, would be involved in the program. I was impressed by the sincerity of some of the people at Neighborhood Services and those representing the Board of Education, both offices having been involved in the planning of the program. An outline of the program's intent was given to me.

> This project was started . . . in an elementary school in the geographical boundaries of the Harlem District of Neighborhood Services. The purpose of the project was to study the effect of an enriched curriculum for two classes of children who live in an isolated, deprived community. The experience of the Board of Education and of Neighborhood Services seemed to point to the fact that in such communities there are a large number of children who begin their school experience with average to excellent academic achievement, good attendance and full participation in all activities, but by the time these children reach fifth grade a marked, steady deterioration frequently sets in which depreciates scores on intelligence tests, destroys interest, and creates a corrosive lack of respect for authority and education. Junior high schools and high schools which the elementary school children eventually attend are plagued by dropouts, truancy, open defiance, and delinquency.
> Because of the complexity of these problems and of the fact that their roots lie in the child's early experiences, the Harlem District Office of Neighborhood Services was called in by the Board of Education to assist in working out the project. Education and casework were thereby joined in a unified approach to understand these children and plan for the program which it was hoped would lead to the prevention of the predicated problems.[2]

I liked this statement because it did not blame the child for school failure; it suggested, in fact, that "deterioration" takes place as the child proceeds through the school, indicating the belief that school practice has something to do with this. Thus, I looked forward to the opening of school and my new class.

---

[1] "Neighborhood Services" will be the name used in place of the actual name by which the agency was known.
[2] Personal communication from the Neighborhood Services Director (June 24, 1959).

MEETING THE CHILDREN

Class 5-4, or Project Class as it was known, had been given a new room to go with its teacher. The administration at Harlem School was hopeful that the class would get back to "normal" under my direction. I myself was anxious to see what I might accomplish with the group. I checked the record cards on the children and found some interesting data. The reading levels of the children were from second grade to fifth grade, a three-year differential. IQ scores were of similar latitude. It was obvious to me that a uniform approach would be inappropriate, but there was something more interesting, I found. The children had never had a white teacher in their time at Harlem School, nor had they ever had a male teacher. Thus, I presented for them an entirely new image. I was not certain at first what this might mean in my relationship to them.

Shortly after the term began, I found that social workers from Neighborhood Services came into class unannounced quite frequently, arousing the children, who would flock around them. This happened no matter what we had been doing in class at the time. After several such instances I began to feel peripheral to the children's personal interests. They had come to associate the members of Neighborhood Services with parties and special trips, and seemed to regard me as an interloper. After awhile I felt that the children were attempting to show that they could "defeat" me as they had defeated their previous teacher. I also found that Harlem School officials really regarded the special project as a "pain in the neck." They were tired of meetings with numerous other officials and did not want to be bothered by parents, whom they felt to be nonprofessionals and irrelevant in school affairs. They thought the project had gotten out of hand and had prevailed too much on their time. Mr. Green openly told me that he wished the project would be terminated. When I attended meetings with Neighborhood Services personnel and school officials, Mr. Green prompted me to say that I had to attend classes at the university, so the meetings would be cut short. And it was quite clear that a coolness existed between Harlem School people and Neighborhood Services. Each, it turned out, thought the other was not contributing adequately to the project. The program was better in its conceptualization than in actual practice. There would be a much more involved task for me, I realized, than I had previously thought.

Shortly thereafter I allowed myself to get involved in a classroom incident that was to compound my problems for a time to come. It occurred relatively early in my relationship to Project Class. Mr. Ives from Neighborhood Services had come to visit the class. The children knew him well and liked him. He announced the scheduling for a party to come soon. After gathering around him, the children were returning to their seats. Accidentally Gill and Bernice bumped one another. It did not take more than a moment before the "sounding" began. Bernice started: "Get out of my way, you shiny bean."

"Who you talking to, you African?" responded Gill.

"Don't call me an African," said Bernice. "You better get your lies straight. You think you're so bad. You think you're white."

"I ain't white, but you're black," said Gill.

"Yeah?" answered Bernice. "Bet it's so hot in your house that the rats carry canteens."

"So what?" Gill came back. "Last week your mother was a virgin."

It was too late for me to stop things. I tried to intercede, but the last remark had really aroused Bernice. She was an orphan living with an aunt, and she felt that Gill's last remark was unwarranted. She pulled a sharp-pointed compass from her desk and rushed at Gill. He avoided her rush and threw her to the floor. He punched her eye repeatedly, egged on by classroom onlookers, before I could pull him off. When I did, he shouted: "Get your motherfuckin' white hands off me!"

The remark simply was made in excitement; it did not stir me. But I was concerned about Bernice. She cried and was even more enraged. She clawed at me as I tried to comfort her. In the meantime Gill drew his fists to a fighting position and dared me, "C'mon, I ain't afraid of you." I was caught in the middle of a situation that seemed absurd. In trying to break up a fight, I was being challenged by the antagonists. It was difficult to think my way out of this predicament. And Gill was unrelenting. He was tall and strong, and knew he could fight. His temper had overcome him, and sweat poured from his face while his chest heaved with excitement.

Finally Wilma and Nancy escorted Bernice to the bathroom to wash her eye. I returned to my desk and asked Gill to go out for a drink of water and to calm down. He was unrelenting, however, and wanted only to engage me in his anger. He pressed his challenge, and I felt that if I did not meet it, I would lose the whole group—perhaps for good. I walked up to him, and he swung wildly at me. I grabbed his arms and held him against the wall. He struggled very hard, but said nothing. He was quite strong, and I admired his effort. He made no excuses for my having constrained him and soon relented. I asked him if I had hurt him. He said, "You can't hurt me, man." I then asked if he felt I had been wrong in my actions, but he did not answer. When I released him, he went outside the door and remained there until dismissal time. The rest of the class sat in a hush until it was time to leave. My initiation into Project Class had reached its emotional peak.

The following week Gill's mother came to visit me. She had been president of the PTA at Harlem School and was active in school affairs. She was known to be very interested in the education of her children. Other children had told her about the incident with Gill, and she wanted to talk to me about it. She was not angry over the encounter, but made it clear that she opposed dealing with children physically. I agreed and tried to explain what had happened in class. She said that she did not blame me for my actions, but she wanted to make certain that Gill would not find himself at a disadvantage in my class over what occurred. It seemed that Gill had originally been in class 3-1 when the project started and had been placed in 5-4 because he was regarded as a discipline problem. She knew he was bright and did not want his occasional aggressive behavior to thwart him in his studies. I agreed that I would try hard to befriend him and to seek the best in him. Our conversation ended on this positive note. I resolved not just to reach Gill, but the other children as well. The understanding of Gill's mother and her encouraging posture were crucial to me at that point. She must be credited with support of me at a time when it was needed. Had she been angry, I would have found it extremely difficult to reverse the trend in class 5-4.

The incident did not end with the visit from Mrs. Victor (Gill's mother), however. The next week a delegation of three parents came to see me. They had been told of the incident and wanted to discuss if it were wise that I continue as the teacher of the class. They said they knew that the project had not really helped their children yet, but they did not want them to have a teacher who would not be concerned about the children. Perhaps, they said, a black teacher would understand the children better. I pointed out that the children had had black teachers in the past and still had not functioned as they might have. Then I asked, in turn, if they as parents would be willing to work together with me in effecting better classroom learning. Eventually they agreed. I told them I would remove myself as the teacher of the children, if at the end of the school year they felt I had not fulfilled their expectations. It was an unusual agreement because I was virtually submitting myself to their scrutiny, rather than to the scrutiny of school officials. Thus, I hoped, they were being offered a small voice in their children's education.

The next day I told the children of my informal pact with the parents. I told them in addition that I wanted to involve them in the agreement. We were supposed to remain together for two years until they would be graduated after the sixth grade. However, I would ask for reassignment after the fifth grade if the children desired it. They were surprised by this offer, though its implication could not immediately be known to them. I was attempting to involve them in their own fate at Harlem School. Their lives were being shaped, and I thought they ought to have a hand in that shaping.

I knew these gestures would be rather empty if 5-4 and I did not try to do things differently. I wanted to seek new approaches to instructing them, but I also had to know them better. I tried to identify the informal clusters and cliques in the classroom. If I could work within the social structure, I thought, I would be more effective. Then too, I had to discover the learning strengths of individual children and to find out as much as possible about their out-of-school lives. Neighborhood Services had gathered considerable material on the children's family lives, so I arranged to discuss each child with social workers from the agency. We met during lunch hours for several weeks and sometimes after school. When I learned all I could, I began informal tours of the neighborhood with some of the children. They delighted in acting as guides and informing me of the places of interest, the good restaurants, where one could "play the numbers," and who was who in the informal structure. Sometimes bits of information were gathered informally. For example, on one of our walks during lunchtime Donny pointed to an open window where a man sat with an infant in his lap and said, "Hey, man, that's my father." I responded, "But you don't live there, do you?" "I know," Donny said, "but that's still my father." I realized that Donny saw nothing unusual about this. He said he saw his father very often and had many good times with him, even though he himself lived with his mother and an older sister.

On occasion we encountered parents or godparents; many relationships the children had to others were revealed on these tours. I got a sense of the children's range of activities and a sense of neighborhood style. These walks became part of my learning experiences, with the children as the instructors. It drew us closer together, the incident with Gill no longer being mentioned by anyone. In the classroom I tried to turn their affinity for debate into an instructional pattern. We had many open discussions and debates which we tape-recorded. On one such occasion I played the role of a bigot and argued in behalf of racial superiority. The children's feelings were quite clear and their thinking was astute on this subject. They even defined the limits of neighborhood by where the black population ended and the white population began. They were much more knowledgeable than one might have thought. On one of our recorded sessions they showed this unmistakably. The theme was "educational procedures." I asked the following: "If you had the means to improve education at Harlem School, or in Project Class, what would you do? What would you consider important?"[3]

ERNIE started: "The first thing, I think, is that a teacher should teach what the children like. If a kid don't want to learn 'two and two,' he isn't going to learn it."

TEACHER: "Don't you think it's a teacher's job to teach what a child is supposed to know?"

DEBORAH: "The first thing a teacher has to learn is understanding of the children, to have confidence in them."

ERNIE: "And the teacher should be aware that most children like to learn new things. Then they'll go home and learn more about it on their own, you know?"

TEACHER: "Let's speak to this. It's found that children here are from one to two years behind in their work. Are teachers doing their job? Let's talk about the factors involved."

WILMA: "I don't think it depends on the teacher that much. If a kid wants to learn, he'll learn."

TEACHER: "You think, regardless of teachers, a child who wants to learn will learn?"

VINCENT: "But I think a teacher should always teach on grade level; not present subjects that are for junior high school or something."

NANCY: "I disagree with Wilma, in a way. Sometimes a child wants to learn, but they don't get it right away. It just don't take up there [pointing to her head]."

---

[3] A copy of this discussion is recorded on tape. The entire discussion is not reported, but that which is reported occurred as given, with only very slight editing to improve the flow of content.

DONNY: "I think the teacher should teach the things he thinks a pupil should know, and what not."

WILMA: "What I meant when I said a pupil will learn it when he wants to learn it . . . . like, you take Gill; he wants to learn real bad. He got more confidence in himself."

TEACHER: "You mean there are differences among pupils: a child will have ability in one subject, while another child will have ability in another subject."

EVERETT: "Like you said, you know, you sat Gill next to me because you said we were bright, or something. Maybe, sometimes, it's better to sit the smart people next to the dumb people, and they might improve a little bit."

DEBORAH: "If I was the teacher and I had bright people in the class, I would put the bright people up in the front and let the ones who want to sleep stay in the back."

TEACHER: "You are all arguing, I think, for a certain kind of grouping; a separation or mingling of certain kinds of children. How about the teacher? What about the neighborhood? How about parents and school officials? Is there anything we should know about them that might help us with our problem?"

DONNY: "My mother says you either come here to learn or don't come at all."

TEACHER: "What makes children not want to learn?"

EVERETT: "Well, they probably have trouble at home. It keeps their mind off their work."

TEACHER: "If the teacher knew about this, would it help?"

EVERETT: "It might."

TEACHER: "How can the teacher find out?"

EVERETT: "He could talk to the child at lunchtime and discuss it with him."

NANCY: "I disagree with Everett. Suppose the child likes the parents, but the parents don't like the child? Suppose the teacher calls the child up about it, but the child just don't want to discuss it—then what do you do?"

TEACHER: "Yes, there is a problem of treading on personal ground."

WILMA: "I don't have a perfect family, I know. I have trouble with my mother, and she has trouble with me, because I'm no angel. I think that has something to do with my school problems, too. I can't get my mother to come to school because she's always going to my sister's school. (She quit school, that dope! Oh, excuse me. That's off the subject.) I think if the teacher and the parent could get together—and the child—and talk their problems out to each other, this whole school would be a better school."

TEACHER: "Do you think teachers and parents show enough interest in doing this?"

NANCY and WILMA: "No!"

I listened to that tape recording many times, and it taught me much. It was a discussion by ten- and eleven-year-olds, but it had the earmarks of a college class in educational foundations of learning. The children had touched on several educational concepts: motivation, children's readiness, subject relevance, pupil needs, family background, teachers' styles, comprehension, and grouping. Obviously, it seemed to me, to involve their ideas in classroom procedure would be a good idea in Project Class.

After several months a picture of the children emerged more clearly. There was an apparent pattern of organization in the classroom, with each child representing a distinct temperament and personality. I too was part of this social structure. I realized that the maintenance of learning—and classroom control—hinged on providing an outlet for each temperamental type. The in-class division of labor would have to allow for the personal expression of each child. I sought to foster this not only on an individual level, but within the subgroupings of children manifest in the classroom. It was discernible that each child had emotional ties to other children in the group. These attachments, I thought, had to be exploited to enhance learning and self-esteem among the children. I drew up capsule descriptions of the children and arranged each child in my mind according to his affiliations.

CARL is an extremely attractive child with a winning way about him. He is small and not physically strong, but he tries to bully others in the class. He fights frequently and has been regarded as a major discipline problem at Harlem School. He seemingly defies the teacher to teach him anything, yet he daily accompanies the teacher to his car, often in silence, appearing to enjoy the image he feels he conveys to others that he is the teacher's friend. Despite his nonchalance, he asks often if the teacher likes him. He sings in class at inopportune moments, as if to attract attention to himself. He is frequently late to school, although he is seen near the school well before the time he is to arrive each day. This seems to be a means by which he gains the teacher's attention. He is reported by Neighborhood Services to have said that he likes the teacher because "he doesn't hit me like my father does." In reading he is assigned to the remedial class. His IQ is 86.

DEMOS is one of two Puerto Rican children in the class. He is very quiet and attentive in class. He speaks Spanish at home and has no difficulty handling English. He frequently reports that his father closely checks his schoolwork at home. He has an older sister at Harlem School who is reported as a fine student. Because he is so quiet, it sometimes appears that he is "scared" of the teacher. His reading level is third grade. His IQ is 97.

DONNY is powerfully built and an exceptional athlete at his age. As a result he is often seen with older boys outside the school with whom he plays ball. He reads all he can about sports, frequently asking for the teacher's newspaper to check scores and trends. He at first gave little interest to his work in class, until the teacher informed him that most professional athletes in professional football and basketball are college graduates. This impressed him with the need to do well in school. He lives with his mother and an older sister, who is a nurse. He is a most meticulous dresser and a very handsome boy. He is never late to school. His IQ is 91 and he reads at a third-grade level, also being assigned to the remedial reading class. He had been reported as a behavior problem, but is no problem of this kind in Project Class.

ERNIE lives in the same building as does Donny. He is apparently in awe of the teacher, appearing embarrassed when he is caught "staring." He smiles easily and works with confidence when given assignments he can accomplish easily. If he gets stuck in his classwork, he is disposed toward sadness and withdrawal. He is very conscious of the girls in class and likes to work with them on his assignments. His mother has been active in the affairs of Project Class. His father too keeps close tabs on his work. His IQ is 93 and he reads at third-grade level.

FRANK is the "model" student. He has an unusual capacity to stick to his work until the results satisfy him. He is constantly pursuing a subject to its conclusion in his mind. He frequently asks to sit alone so that he can work without interruption. He seems indefatigable in his studies. His mother and father work during the day, and he must assume many of the household chores. An aunt is frequently mentioned as being an occasional member of the household. His IQ is 93 and he reads at a third-grade level.

GILL is the strongest boy in the class and the tallest. He is the most "adult" among the boys. He has a sharp grasp of black-white relationships and is very outspoken about them. His mother's involvement in the PTA is also reflected in his point of view. He is a "militant" person even at his young age. His father is a clergyman. He likes to talk to the teacher privately about serious matters, often coming to the classroom during lunchtime to do so, even though this is "against regulations." He follows his schoolwork as if he has a mission to accomplish. At first he followed few directions and cursed and fought frequently with the others. He is very interested in different world peoples and often asks for books about them. His IQ is 100, and he reads at third-grade level.

EVERETT is quiet and reserved in manner, but is very alert. He is exceedingly bright and is probably the best student in the class. However, he often appears troubled in class. His father is not regularly in the home, and his mother frankly speaks about the problems she has in taking care of the family. There is a sister and a grandmother in the home too. He often starts his assignments well after the others are under way, as if to accept a handicap for himself. He continually illuminates class discussion by his contributions. He is well liked, particularly by the girls who think he is a handsome boy. His IQ is 103, and he reads at grade level.

HERMAN has been characterized as a slow learner. He does at times appear to be lethargic and detached. However, he is really a bit shy and not lethargic, nor is he slow. He lives with his mother and two older sisters. He is interested in sports and different places, often asking "unanswerable" questions of the teacher, such as: "How long is the Columbia River?" and "What is the fourth largest city in Russia?" He has a low initiation of activity rate, but is usually asked by the boys to join their activities. His reading is at third-grade level, and his IQ is 83.

ISAAC is unintentionally deceptive in his ways. He seems to be slow-thinking and uninformed, yet he is quite bright. He enjoys the reputation of having the best handwriting in the class and spends unusual amounts of time seeing to it that his work is "just right." If his work is not completed on time, he frankly states that he did not have enough time to make it appear as he wants it to. He is a prolific storyteller, rivaling Donny for honors in this activity. His mother has expressed surprise that he is doing well in school. Previous teachers have described him as a "problem." His IQ is 107, and he reads at fourth grade level.

JAMES was not originally in Project Class, but came to it from another school in the fifth grade. He has fitted in well and has become friendly with the other children. The decision to enter him in 5-4 was another indication by school administration not to treat the class as "special" any longer. He enjoys drawing caricatures of others in the class, the teacher being the most frequent object of his attentions. His father is a superintendent of a nearby tenement, and his mother has expressed frequent interest in his studies. He is a good athlete and has become friendly with Donny as a result. He reads at third-grade level. There is no indication on the record card of any IQ score.

LEONARDO is one of eight children. He is the other Puerto Rican child in the class. He too speaks Spanish at home but is fluent in English. He is the class "rusher," always completing his work first, whether it is correctly done or not. He says frequently that he likes to get out of the house, for if he hangs around, he gets caught with all kinds of chores. He likes sports and is a good athlete. He is always early to school in order to play ball in the yard before class starts. His parents are friendly with the parents of Demos. His IQ is 89, and he reads at third-grade level.

STANLEY is quite shy. He does not like to argue or fight. Sometimes he is picked on by the others, kiddingly, as if they want to draw him out and encourage him to "stick up for himself." His mother is very active in Project Class affairs and spends much time at the school. His IQ is 79 and he reads on third-grade level.

Of the twelve boys in Project Class, Carl, Gill, and Isaac had been considered major discipline problems in the past. Only Carl proved to be a problem in 5-4. He simply did not respond to my academic promptings. Neighborhood Services revealed that he was often severely beaten at home. I knew him to be very capable, but could not convince him to try. It was as if he were determined to outlast all my efforts.

The girls were even more varied as a group than the boys. There was great diversity in temperament, academic performance, and intragroup interaction.

BERNICE was basically a quiet child, often moody and contemplative. When aroused, she had a violent temper. She and her brothers were orphans, living with an aunt and older cousin. She often fought with Susan who also had an aggressive temperament when stimulated. Bernice was friendly with Donna, often sharing candy and jokes. She tries to get Charlotte into "trouble" by playing tricks on her. She has an IQ of 96 and is on third grade in reading level.

CAMILLE is the oldest child in the class, having entered 5-4 from another school. Her record card shows that she attended five different schools the previous year. She has been retained once in grade in the past. Her godmother reports that Camille's mother is only thirteen years her senior. It is also reported that Camille is frequently beaten at home. Indeed, she often appears tired and bruised in class. However, she is the "toughest" child in the group, even the boys remaining aloof in her presence. Interestingly she is a constant companion to Darlene, also a new child, who is the smallest child in the class. Her father is unknown to her. Her IQ is 90; her reading level is second grade.

CHARLOTTE is an extremely pleasant child, having a most friendly disposition. She is rarely angered by anything and has an easy smile, though she is often the butt of classroom pranks by others. She is the "slowest" learner in the class, but is not upset by things she does not know. Curiously Norma, one of the brighter girls, is a close friend of hers. She is also friendly with Bernice, Darlene, Donna, and Susan. Charlotte's mother often speaks to the teacher and is very similar to Charlotte in temperament and manner. Charlotte's father works for the transit authority and reportedly treats her very well as her stepfather. She is in the remedial reading class, and her measured IQ is 75.

DARLENE is the smallest child in the class and looks even younger than her eleven years. She often remains at home in bad weather and is quiet and shy. She needs frequent support and encouragement in her classwork. Camille seems to assume a protective role with her, which gives her confidence. The two get along very well. Her IQ is 84, and she reads at third-grade level.

DEBORAH has been transferred into Project Class because she was regarded as a behavior problem by her previous teacher. She is well behaved in class, however, but seems to have a propensity for calling out at all times; apparently, this is what earned her the label of "behavior problem." Little is known of her out-of-school life because she is not part of the casework load at Neighborhood Services as yet. Her IQ is 98; she reads at fourth-grade level.

DONNA is the oldest of ten children, all born to the same parents. She is often absent from school and at first seemed to have little interest in school. After a house helper was arranged for by Neighborhood Services, her classwork picked up noticeably. She often brings pictures of movie stars to class and carefully looks them over. She often says she "wants to be left alone." Her reading level is third grade and her IQ is 94.

HORTENSE almost never speaks in class. She lives alone with her mother. She is friendly with Inez with whom she shares candy, stories, and gossip. At first, she said she had not learned anything in Project Class and wished she were in a different class. Though she seems unconcerned about her work, she always does it as required. Her mother was one of those who came to visit the teacher after the incident with Gill. Her IQ is 93, and she reads at third-grade level.

INEZ is one of four sisters, all attending Harlem School. She does not try hard in class, but her older sister is reported as an excellent student. Though she has few friends in the class, she is not disliked. Her parents frequently come to the Saturday school sessions. Her IQ is 82; her reading level is third grade.

NANCY is the most popular of the girls. She has a high interaction rate and seems to talk at one time or another to everyone in the class on a given day. She is very attractive and outspoken. She lives with her mother and grandmother. She does not know her father. She herself is often seen taking care of a niece. She is very friendly and spirited. Her IQ is 80, and her reading level is fourth grade.

NORMA, though very quiet in class, is very astute. She often understands subtleties the other children do not grasp. Much brighter than Charlotte, she is nevertheless friendly with her. In discussions of contemporary and historic affairs she shows wide knowledge, apparently reading at home on her own in these subjects. She rarely stirs from her seat and is not demonstrable in her responses. She lives alone with her mother and father. Her IQ is 90. She reads at fourth-grade level.

SUSAN is very active in class and has been described as a behavior problem since first grade. Social workers from Neighborhood Services report that she is harshly punished at home. She is believed to be the offspring of her father and her father's niece. It is also reported that Susan knows this. In the presence of her father she is very subdued. At other times she is assertive and very aggressive. She defies the teacher and frequently fights with other children. She is, however, very winning when she wants to be. She is in the remedial reading class and has an IQ of 81.

WILMA is the brightest and, according to the boys, the prettiest girl in the class. She lives with her mother and an older sister. It is to be said that her grace is striking. Though she considered Project Class a "dumb" class at first, she says she likes it now. At times she is shy with the teacher but says she likes him. Neighborhood Services reports that her sister is known to be a prostitute. Her mother works nights. Wilma is said to know of her sister's activities. She spends most of the day on her own, waiting for her mother to return from work in the early morning. Her IQ measured 120, and she reads at grade level.

Together the children formed a group that had a discernible structure (see Figures 1, 2, and 3). There were major lines of influence that were predicated on school activities and on outside contacts as well. Though the school arranged and assembled children in classes on the bases of scholastic aptitude and related criteria, in individual classes there appeared a variety of subgroupings grounded in other aspects of their behavior; particularly, the social structure was derived of the interaction patterns among the children. From these was derived a system of sentiments and values which were

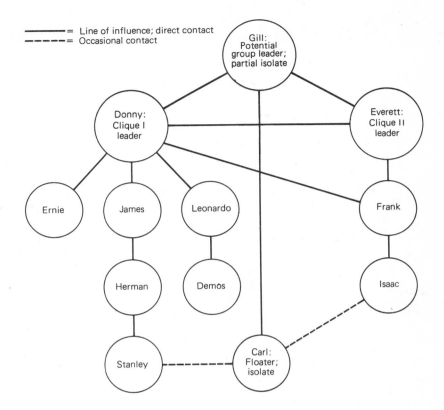

Figure 1. Project Class boys: Social organization

also extensions of community beliefs and activities. I knew that the viability of any classroom culture system resided in its ability to tolerate and give expression to the diverse personality structures of the children, especially when differing personalities contribute in special ways to subject and content transmission. In fact, certain subject areas fostered certain personality types and temperamental styles, and the teacher who can link these is the more successful one. This requires a somewhat different view of what curriculum and instruction mean. It had taken me several months, but I had finally arrived at a workable base or model for instruction in 5-4.

Teaching is, before anything else, a set of social relationships with children. As such, one has to work with the social groupings the children form among themselves. They were not always overtly aware of it, but they assembled into groups on the bases of learning style, personal friendship, special interest, and personality characteristics. As the teacher I had to be willing to assume for myself at different times much of their personal styles. Among the boys, as an illustration, there were several themes regulating

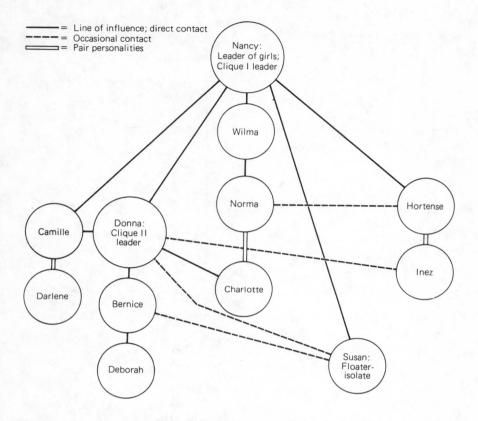

= Line of influence; direct contact
= Occasional contact
= Pair personalities

Figure 2. *Project Class girls: Social organization*

their behavior and associations. Two major cliques resulted from this. Ability to fight and argue was one theme. Here, Gill was the acknowledged leader. He had already shown his mettle in standing up to the teacher earlier. He argued with anyone when he thought he was justified. Donny, a demonstrative storyteller, often captured the group with his stories of the exploits of older friends. He was also a fine athlete, another mark of status among the boys. He was the leader of one subgroup in the class. Membership in this grouping, clique I, also included Ernie, Leonardo (also a good athlete), James, Herman, Stanley, and Demos (who shared a close relationship with Leonardo).

Besides ability at fighting, sports, and debate, an additional attribute among the boys was school performance. Here clique II was in evidence. It consisted of Everett, the clique leader, Frank, and Isaac. Gill also interacted with this group. All of these boys were good students. Carl was neither a good athlete nor a good student; thus, he shared only sporadic contact with the two cliques. He would have been a more complete isolate, had he no contact with Gill, the general leader. In fact, Gill's interaction pattern in-

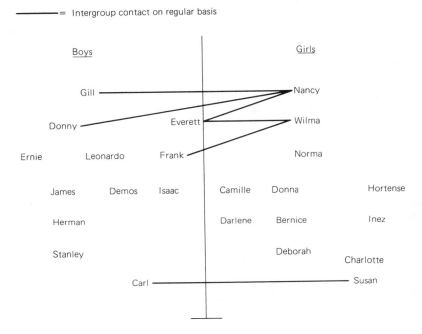

——————= Intergroup contact on regular basis

Boys   Girls

Gill   Nancy

Donny   Everett   Wilma

Ernie   Leonardo   Frank   Norma

James   Demos   Isaac   Camille   Donna   Hortense

Herman   Darlene   Bernice   Inez

Stanley   Deborah
                                          Charlotte

Carl   Susan

Figure 3.   Project Class: Intergroup (boys and girls) organization

volved him with all the boys, but he often preferred to be alone. He initiated activity for all of them and could easily be approached by them when he felt like doing so. These were definite signs of leadership status (Homans 1950: 415–440), and except for his self-imposed isolation at times, Gill would have been instrumental in almost all the boys' activities.

Among the girls there were similar definable groupings. Guiding themes of behavior for them related to the sharing of candy and secrets, argument, rope jumping, flirting with the boys, and classroom performance. Nancy was the overall leader of the girls and the leader of clique I, which included Wilma, Norma, and sometimes Charlotte (who shared a pairs relationship with Norma, but did not share the characteristics which bound the girls of clique I together). This clique formed the "smartest" group of girls, excepting Charlotte, who was regarded as not bright. Nancy, Norma, and Wilma were excellent students; and Nancy and Wilma were the only girls the boys cared to interact with regularly.

Clique II was headed by Donna, who was the most active candy-getter. Other members were Bernice, Deborah, Camille, Darlene, and Charlotte, who shared candy with Donna. Susan shared candy with Donna and occasionally fought with Bernice; otherwise, she was isolated from the girls. Clique II was a group which was frequently in debate, at play together, or sharing secrets and candy. The girls who were members were less than avid in their studies. Within the clique Camille and Darlene shared a pairs relationship, always doing things together.

Hortense and Inez formed another pair-personality relationship. They were separate from the other girls except when Inez shared candy with Donna, and Hortense shared secrets with Norma. Neither Hortense nor Inez was as vocal as the other girls; neither was each girl as good a rope jumper as the rest. And they were not as good in their studies as were the girls in clique I. If they did not have each other, they would have been isolates, as was Susan, who had only partial contact with Donna and Bernice. Nancy was the only one who really interacted with Susan.

Quite apparently Nancy was a key person in the social organization of the girls. She was also prominent in intergroup contact with the boys, particularly with Gill, Donny, and Everett. Wilma too had a pattern of interaction with the boys. Thus, Gill, Donny, Everett, Nancy, and Wilma emerged as key persons in the class social structure. Significantly they were all good or excellent students, which related directly to the purpose for which the larger group was to come together in school. It left little doubt in my mind that I would have to use their influence in effecting positive social and learning conditions in Project Class.

As the organizational pattern of the class shows, however, Carl and Susan were the most estranged from the group. In addition they were not good students. I had to change this, I knew. There was no doubt a connection between class social standing and academic standing. The cycle of failure had to be broken for these two children. Paradoxically it was difficult to influence social standing without first influencing academic standing and vice versa. Carl and Susan and I were caught in a difficult problem. It was my most important task to reach them. However, I was not able to do so. At the end of the fifth grade Carl and Susan left Project Class. Camille left too, once again moving to another neighborhood.

CLASS 6-4

Much had happened in my first year with Project Class. It also was the end of my third year at Harlem School and was the point at which I felt confident of my teaching. My experience with Opportunity Class and Project Class had finally come to a meaningful confluence. I now felt that I knew how to look at children and how to work with them. There had been many anxious moments for the children in 5-4, but we had consolidated ourselves into a working unit, ready for the sixth grade. I had come to know them better than any group of children I had taught. We saw our school lives linked together. I had come to know most of the parents of the children and a good part of the neighborhood. I was convinced that the sixth grade would be my best effort.

I did, nevertheless, have some misgivings. Though it was agreed that

I would continue with the children, I knew I had failed Carl and Susan. It was not enough to say that I would be able to reach them if they were not removed from the class. But nothing could be done. Neighborhood Services reported that Susan's father had requested she be entered in a different class. The agency attributed his discontent to what Susan's father called "prying" into his personal affairs by several social workers. He did not want his personal life "bared," it was felt, because the suspicion that Susan was the daughter of his niece might be verified. I knew Susan was bright, and I knew she faced many problems a child her age should have been free from. I wondered what her later life would be like. I hoped she would grow up fast and that she would leave the conditions that weighed so heavily upon her in her young life.

Carl, toward the end of fifth grade, had become a constant truant. On many days he would meet me at my car, not having been to school the entire day. When I asked if his parents knew he stayed out from school, he answered that they "didn't care." On occasion when he did come to class, he said he knew that I did not like him and that he hated the class. Mr. Green wanted to retain him in the fifth grade, but I asked that he be sent on, perhaps to another teacher if this would keep him from being left back. It was agreed. However, Carl did not get on with his new teachers; he came to visit me often in the sixth grade and was switched several times to different classes for being a behavior problem. I wondered many times since then if Mr. Green was happy that Carl was not successful at Harlem School, for he came to me many times with an "I-told-you-so" attitude. I wondered too if any of the small successes I had with other children could make up for my failure with Carl. I do not think so.

Camille also left our class; once agile and energetic, she appeared weary and resigned to her fate as rootless and unhappy. Never had she been able to stay in one place very long, having attended more than a dozen schools at her young age. Her case illustrated poignantly what many poor people must endure. I hoped her physical strength would help her, but it was her psychological strength that would determine whether she would withstand. Darlene, who was lonely for a time after Camille left, I knew, would hope hard for her.

Several other changes took place at Harlem School and Neighborhood Services during that fourth year of my teaching. Class 6-1, the other class in the experiment, received a new teacher, their former teacher thinking that three years with the same class was enough. She had done an outstanding job with the class and simply wanted to give the group the benefit of another teacher in their graduating year. The new teacher was highly regarded as well. At the end of the year 6-1 emerged as the top class in the school.

Having retired, Mr. Hecht was replaced as principal. The new principal at Harlem School was a woman who took an active interest in the Project Classes; however, her first year was one of becoming accustomed to her new assignment. Thus, her role was more one of encouragement than of involvement in the experiment.

At Neighborhood Services several key people left for other positions. A new director had been recently assigned, and some shifts took place within the agency. The monthly meetings that used to take place at Harlem School stopped. The social workers did not visit at the school any longer, though some still went to the homes of the children. The Saturday school program dissipated as well. For the most part 6-4 was like any other class now. There was an important exception, however: this was our second year together; the breaking-in period was long over. The children and I knew what to expect from one another, our strong and weak points. Our class was also smaller than most, with only twenty-one children now that three children had left the class. It offered an opportunity at classroom life that was not usual for Harlem School. The joining of casework and instruction had given immense insight into the children. And my discovery of the classroom social structure—the organization of activities—allowed me to fit instruction to the social pattern. Our efforts became joint efforts, involving children in groups where possible. The subgroupings bound children in unified attempts, individual gains being seen as gains for the group and the class as a whole. There was no child who did not importantly surpass previous achievements; every child improved noticeably in all academic areas in the sixth grade. The effort was mostly theirs.

My involvement in the Saturday school program had brought me into contact with the parents and allowed us to share the experiences of the children and our own private lives. I had, for example, innumerable discussions with Charlotte's mother on the trials of bringing up a newborn baby. Children had been born to her and my wife at about the same time, so we compared the respective progress of the infants each Saturday. In similar fashion I came to know the other parents in an informal manner. No presumed distance between us was allowed to form. Our common interest was the children. They formed the point of tangency between school and home.

Other events helped weld class 6-4 into a confident and aware group. On several of our trips out of school I took along my three-year-old son. The girls were entirely in charge of him. The amazing expertise in child care which they brought to bear revealed them as extremely capable. Many of them had been in charge of younger children throughout their school lives, and they enjoyed the chance to chaperone my son on some of our brief excursions.

The boys and I had drawn closer together in several ways. We went swimming together at a neighborhood community center pool near Harlem School. This put us together in "man-to-man" activities. Many teachers informed me that this was "unprofessional behavior" on my part, but the swimming was more attractive than their words were coercive. They were "shocked" that I would shower and dress with the children. Some even asserted that I would be "contaminated" swimming in the same pool with the children.

On one of our outings we went to a night baseball game at Yankee Stadium. As a matter of fact my final acceptance by Gill came about at this event. Frank, Everett, Herman, Donny, Wilma, and Gill were along with me at the game. We were returning to the neighborhood after midnight and had stopped for some ice cream. I decided I would walk each child back to his house, rather than to drive in the network of one-way streets. Gill was the last child remaining and as we entered his street he said, "Don't walk me down the block!" "Why not?" I asked. "I don't want you to," he said. I then told him that I did not care if he wanted to stay out on the street at this late hour, but that his parents would expect that I return home with him at this time of night. "It's not that," Gill said; "It's just that you might not get out the other end of the block. People aren't used to seeing a white man here at night."

I realized that Gill was actually concerned with my well-being, even if the danger he foresaw was not quite so real. Kiddingly I said, "You mean it would be dangerous for me even if people knew I was your teacher?" "Especially if they knew you were my teacher, man," he answered. And we both laughed. I walked him down the block and left him at the stoop to his house. Nothing happened of course, but I knew that Gill and I were friends. I knew I had finally been accepted, and it felt good. Teachers need the acceptance of children as much as children need this from teachers.

Gradually we built new approaches to subject matter in class 6-4, based on the nature of the subject matter, the spatial and temporal aspects of classroom activity, and the personal and social attributes of the children. I tried to be aware of several variables, so to speak, that obtained in the learning situation. I was not motivated by an "individual psychology" approach but by an amalgam of several concerns. First I tried to take into account the relationship of the subject matter to our personal lives, the nature of the community surrounding the school, and the structural aspects of the school itself—socially and physically. I also asked of the children the acceptance of a comparative point of view: How did people in different places and different times do it? Social studies formed the base of our work. Our reading matter was drawn largely from the realities of people's lives; included were myths, folklore, and poetry. We spent little time with formal readers and the outdated books prevalent at Harlem School.

We tried also to interpret as best we could the central modes of inquiry employed in various disciplines. Where we could, we tried to create conditions in the classroom under which the spirit and temperament of representatives of these fields could be simulated. Some activities that had been seen as solitary became group undertakings (arithmetic for example), and some group activities became singular activity (as for instance, social studies inquiry: questionnaire and survey). If we had to rearrange the room, we did so. Individual reading was often set to dramatization by the entire class. Anyone not interested in what was happening at a particular time was not blindly bound to the activity; he could play chess, work on writing a story, construct puzzles, or occupy himself until he was reattracted to what others were doing. There were many days when I gave little or no overt direction to the children. Primary was the opportunity to bring something to conclusion, to personal fulfillment.

These procedures became legitimate outlets for children of different learning styles and differential interests in varying subjects. We had one guideline: no one could act to satisfy himself at the expense of another. Thus, if someone wanted to join an activity, he was not to be denied. Every child had to submit to tutoring from another child in some subject; that is, he had to be willing to work in a group of others for the improvement of particular skills in which he was deficient. Gill helped children in mathematics. Everett and Wilma helped children in reading and formal writing. Norma accepted Charlotte as her personal charge. She did measurably more with her than I could have done. Herman became our geographer, and Frank was a jack-of-all-trades.

Nancy and Donna joined forces to complement one another and to work with the other girls. Bernice appeared to have lost most of her anger, having been considerably influenced by Nancy in personal deportment and appearance. A fight between children became a rarity; when it occurred, it was usually trivial and short-lived—a dispute over a candybar, perhaps. By now the class had gained a sense of group process and group style. This was shown when a new boy was to be entered in the class at midyear. He was Samuel, an extremely powerful child, who at age twelve weighed 180 pounds and stood five feet, eight inches tall. Mr. Green told me that Samuel had been expelled from a neighboring school for having taken a knife to two teachers. It was hoped he might "straighten out" in my class.

The children in Project Class did not challenge Samuel to "prove himself" as ordinarily they would. They let him feel his way gradually until he felt a part of the group. Never, as a result, did Samuel act out in any way. He threatened no one and soon gave indication that he wanted to join in our activities. For two months he showed fine progress in his work, but then he disappeared from class. He was away for almost a month before we decided to find him and get him back to school. The children roamed the neighborhood until they learned that Samuel had gone to work on a fruit truck. They found him and coerced him into coming back to school. When he did return, he told me that he would not remain because he knew he "would not get promoted anyway." I told him that he would be promoted if he joined a classroom group in order to make up for the time he lost. Frank, Gill, and Ernie worked with him, and their efforts were rewarded. Samuel was eventually graduated with the rest of the group and knew that he had made some new friends.

It would be false to imply that everything was just right in Project Class. It was, of course, not so. And perhaps my own "becoming" was transferred by me to the children, so that I wanted to think that they were doing better than was in fact the case. There was some objective evidence of a significant kind, however, that did show the children's accomplishments. This was so, despite the obstructions placed in the way of the children by Harlem School dogma and officials; I was continually cautioned to "follow the curriculum" and not to deviate from prescribed routines. Once the principal, coming to class on an informal visit, requested that I not teach division of fractions, as I had been doing when she arrived. Again, "it's not in the curriculum," she told me. This led later to an interesting extension of our encounter. At midterm in the spring the children in the entire sixth grade were to take a citywide mathematics examination. Class 6-4 did very well. Gill, to everyone's amazement, scored 100 percent on the test. This had not happened at Harlem School in the long memories of teachers and officials. When I informed the principal that division of fractions was included in the examination, she told me that the test could not then be valid. There must be some items a child will miss she told me. I disagreed, but she informed me that she had been in the business of education long enough to know better than I about testing procedures in the elementary school. Finally I asked her if she were unhappy that the children in Project Class had done well on the examination, despite the inclusion of division of fractions. She thought this to be an impertinent question.

The most monumental formal achievement by the children came about when the citywide reading tests were administered. There had been great concern at Harlem School that children not score too low on the test. When the results were tabulated, Project Class surprised everyone. They scored so well that Mr. Green suggested they be retested with another reading instrument. It was not stated, but it was implied that I somehow had something unusual to do with the scores on the examination. (In truth, I did not administer the test; another teacher did.) A version of the New York City Growth in Reading Test was given to the children. However, they equalled their previous scores and were delighted. They felt they had proved beyond doubt what they could do. The improvement they had shown since the beginning of fifth grade was quite impressive (see Table 1 on page 82).

Much of our remaining weeks together, before the children would go on to junior high school, was spent in fostering further outlet for individual expression. Some children tried to write and illustrate their own stories. Others tried to "invent" their own games. One objective was to achieve a social studies game where none of the participants would be a loser, where the objective was to compromise, rather than to vanquish one's opponent. Some interesting attempts were made in initial stages of this undertaking. The children's behavior continued to disprove the myths normally held about them. The only possible pedagogic danger was to expect too much from them, if that is possible to say at all.

The reading tests had indicated that all the children had progressed. The lowest gain was made by Bernice and Charlotte, but even they had gained a year and three months over their fifth-grade reading levels. Donna, Norma, and Frank had gained three years in reading since the start of fifth grade. And Wilma had gained over four years by this estimation—a remarkable performance! These tests were administered before the end of the sixth year. At its end the scores might have been even higher. Theoretically the children as a group were still eight months behind "normal" reading levels after the examination had been given, but they had been one year and six months behind when they had entered fifth grade. Eventually Harlem School officials were satisfied with the results. After the examination Project Class was rarely bothered by trivial school details. We were left alone for the most part.

TABLE 1

METROPOLITAN ACHIEVEMENT TEST, FORM AM (INTERMEDIATE READING TEST).[1]

	Reading (comprehension)	Vocabulary	Average	Fifth-Grade Reading
Demos	5.3	6.2	5.75	3.0
Donny	5.0	5.7	5.35	3.1
Ernie	6.2	5.4	5.8	3.1
Everett	6.7	6.9	6.8	5.0
Frank	5.8	6.9	6.35	3.3
Gill	4.9	6.6	5.75	3.0
Herman	5.4	5.8	5.6	3.0
Isaac	6.2	5.8	6.0	4.1
James	4.8	5.2	5.0	3.0
Leonardo	4.5	4.8	4.65	3.1
Stanley	5.2	6.1	5.65	3.0
Bernice	4.5	4.5	4.5	3.2
Charlotte	3.0	3.8	3.4	2.1
Darlene	5.1	4.9	5.0	3.0
Deborah	5.4	6.2	5.8	4.0
Donna	6.7	5.6	6.25	3.3
Hortense	6.1	5.3	5.7	3.1
Inez	4.6	4.5	4.55	2.9
Nancy	5.7	5.9	5.8	4.0
Norma	7.2	7.3	7.25	4.1
Wilma	10.5	8.2	9.35	5.0
Class	5.67	5.79	5.735	3.4

[1] Also included are the fifth-grade reading levels for comparison.

From *Metropolitan Achievement Tests, Form Am/Intermediate Reading Test* (Tarrytown-on-Hudson, New York: World Book Company, 1960). Grade levels are indicated as follows: whole numbers indicate year of school (grade level), decimals indicate month of school year (ten months to the school year). Thus, a score of 5.7, for example, indicates fifth grade, seventh month (March). Theoretically, to be on grade level upon entering sixth grade, a child should have a score of 6.0.

It was difficult to assess the factors involved in the children's success. No doubt the involvement of Neighborhood Services had played an important part. The special trips and the extracurricular activities (Saturday school) had been important too. Still, I tended to think that the success of instruction is largely settled in the classroom. The discovery of the in-class social organization was the most important factor to me as the teacher of the group—the necessity to discern the units of cooperation among the children. This latter aspect seems to me to be an important factor in all work and associational groupings (J. Brown 1954). This kind of approach is probably relevant with all children at school. It was for me an applied anthropological approach where one regarded the class as the host culture, with the teacher as the change agent.[4] Group and individual needs had to

---

[4] See Niehoff (1966). Here the author deals with processes of change in different cultural settings.

be discovered, and the maintenance of classroom innovation had to eventually be in the hands of the children. This also depended on the discovery of relevant and supportive people in the children's social environment. Such people are sometimes to be found in the school. For Project Class, persons of this kind were to be found at home in certain instances and among Neighborhood Services personnel. Had such people existed within the school administration, the experiment with Project Class would have been that much more successful in the children's behalf. Unhappily Harlem School officials never fully comprehended the potential significance of the program. This may, indeed, suggest the need to involve other kinds of people in school policy and instruction—parents, university people, social welfare workers, and community agents. Of course, a teacher too has to feel supported; then he will be that much more supportive of children.

Many teachers at Harlem School felt, as did the children, frustrated in their work. To be self-propelling, teachers and children need to find reward in the classroom situation, just as the ability to aspire to long-range goals in education requires confidence in the materials and techniques of instruction. But these instruments alone are insufficient. They have to be accompanied by a wider educational philosophy and a more expansive view of who the child is. The basic detriment to positive learning at Harlem School was the view that techniques of instruction are of the first order, over and above an understanding of the children's cultural experience and the means by which they internalize attitudes and skills to cope with their physical and social environment. Curriculum has to be founded on, and grounded in, the latter. Learning has to be applicable in terms of children's existing knowledge. This is not to say that there are not some things that all children must come to know; it is to say that the means by which they come to know these must be compatible with already existing cultural perceptions and methods of personal coping. At Harlem School it was not the children who could not change; more often it was the teachers who would not change.

10 / The explosion of some myths: the children speak

THE MAJOR PERSONAL SUPPORT in teaching comes from the children. The impetus needed to work with them successfully comes from increased knowledge of their personal lives and capabilities. In Project Class, after the children had entered sixth grade, their "emergence" was unmistakable. They had "hit their stride." Their continued gains were limited only by my capacity to stimulate them further. Still, encouragement came not only from them but from their parents as well. I received notes and letters from parents on many occasions, or they would drop in to offer advice and suggestion. At times they sent cookies or cakes to class with the children. Though they were not ordinarily present in the classroom, their efforts helped join us together in working for the children. Gill's mother, for example, sent frequent notes of recognition in teacher behalf.

> Dear Mr. ———
> Words are inadequate to thank you for all the things you have done for Gill.
> Your patience, kindness and worthwhile guidance has captured many of his weak points.
> I sincerely hope he proves that he appreciates this by his actions.
> Teachers Recognition Day is every day with me. Happy Teachers Recognition Day.[1]

Everett's mother too sent frequent notes, often just a sentence or two showing her interest in her son's work. "Just to say hope you have a pleasant vacation for you and your family. My son has learned a lot more than I did when I was his age. Good luck and God bless you."[2]

Charlotte's mother sent letters, even though I frequently saw her after school was over on many days and at Saturday school too.

> Dear Mr. ———
> I am, very happy to say you have done a wonderful job for the children scince you have been, teaching them, and I might say you sertenly have been, very patien and nice trying to help Charlotte with her work.

---

[1] Letter from Gill's mother, May 16, 1961.
[2] Letter from Everett's mother (no date; however, it was written toward the end of the fifth grade for Project Class—June, 1960).

And I apreacate all you have done and I wish I could afford to give you a nice token for the work you have done, with the children.

I am closing, hoping God will bless you.

Yours truly.[3]

I do not think parents realized how instrumental their sentiments were in enhancing my own efforts, nor do I think Harlem School officials realized the strong interest parents had in what was happening at the school. I was convinced that deliberate efforts at involving parents in school policy was imperative for children—particularly, poor children. Giving parents a direct hand in the destiny of their children was very important to them. Those parents who had not enjoyed an extensive formal education needed to know, nevertheless, that they had formidable contributions to make to the formal education of their children. In fact, I believed that many could serve as tutors, storytellers, and craftsmen; sewing, for example, was certainly a craft that parents were expert at, many themselves making clothing for the children. There was a whole inventory of skills that had been passed along by families over the years that could be conveyed to children. The children in turn were often the educative agents in their parents' behalf, bringing home from school various formal skills at reading and writing that some parents had been denied in the rural South and segregated cities from which they came to Harlem. In any case, regular contact between teachers and parents, with specific focus on children's learning, would only help the children. Unfortunately the inclusion of lay people in education is seen by teachers as an invasion of their own expertise and professionalism. Thus, the appearance of parents at Harlem School somehow spelled danger for school officials. They wanted as little to do with parents as possible.

One learned from the parents, nonetheless, even by the letters they sent to school for different reasons. I was able to look at these letters as "evidence" about the children's lives, as related data in researching the best approaches to teaching. When a note was written to me about a problem in school, it gave an insight into what parents considered important for their children.

Dear Mr. —————

My son, Everett, says he has not been getting his lunch because he would not eat his soup. I am on Welfare and hardly have anything at home. In fact today I don't know where our next meal is coming from. I have to borrow and sometimes my friends don't have the money to lend me. My husband is not working and hasn't sent me any money. I hope he can eat today. He had no breakfast because I didn't have it. I only get $20.00 Semi-monthly.

Yours truly.[4]

Notes explaining children's absences gave glimpses into the exigencies of being poor. "Dear Mr. —————, My daughter Wilma was absent from

---

[3] Letter from Charlotte's mother, May 6, 1961.
[4] Letter from Everett's mother, April 12, 1961.

school on Wednesday because she had to get a pair of shoes. Thank you."[5] When welfare checks came, parents tried to outfit their children. Sometimes parents worked at night and had to keep children out of school in the day when they had time to go shopping with them for clothing. In other instances bills had to be paid and children had to watch other children at home. "Dear Mr. —————, Donna is late because I keep her home while I went to pay rent."[6] One could not reprimand children for occasionally being late, for falling asleep in class at times, or for not completing a particular home-work assignment. There were family obligations to be taken care of so fre-quently that no one else could do for them. Under these circumstances it was quite remarkable that the children performed as well as they did in class. And they did well, taking their total lives into account.

Essays and other forms of writing became a major means in class by which the children communicated. They had great verbal ability, and transforming this ability to the written word was a matter of transforming it in their terms, allowing their use of language to be acceptable even when grammatical niceties were absent. Parents' letters had disproved the myth about their disinterest in their children's education. They knew better than anyone else about the debilitating effects of poverty, and they were willing to support any teacher who seemed interested in the welfare of the children. When they remained aloof, it was because they questioned teachers' motives and did not want to intercede in the event this would reflect negatively on their children's chances. Cultural restraints were evident in some cases too. For example, the parent of a pupil might not come to school when summoned because there was self-consciousness about clothing styles, a feeling that one was not properly attired for a school visit. A Puerto Rican mother, as another illustration, might feel constrained to stay out of the limelight, leaving public appearances for the father. Yet, the father might be at work, unable to respond to the teacher's invitation to the school. Here again the teacher had to be willing to judge parents' behavior in terms of the items the parents themselves saw as relevant in their lives. One would need to know some-thing about Puerto Rican subculture if Puerto Rican children were in the class (Padilla 1958). With the children's writing, then, one would have to know something about colloquial and slang expression, not only the proper placement of a part of speech. Releasing the inhibitions of the children was releasing their expressive talents as well. Similarly, relinquishing one's per-sonally held myths about the children released the teacher from his own self-imposed restraints.

In looking at the children in Project Class, other barriers to their real capabilities were removed. It was found that some of the best students were from homes where fathers were absent or only temporarily at home. Wilma and Nancy did not know their fathers; Everett and Donny saw their fathers intermittently. What was the validity of the assertion that children could

---

[5] Letter from Wilma's mother, February 16, 1961.
[6] Letter from Donna's mother, February 17, 1961.

not learn when fathers were not in the home? A father's absence was more a negative influence on the teacher who thought this to be an impediment to learning and then acted on this belief in ways that hindered the children. There was no intractable sameness among the children. Project Class showed clearly the wide range of personality types among them. The fact that the children shared poverty in common did not mean that their reactions in the classroom were uniform or in any way immutable. It simply meant that there existed for them a differential in the means toward fulfillment of some of the same aspirations heralded by the larger, dominant culture. Being poor had put severe restrictions on material and social attainment, but not on personal preference or temperamental variety. Even in the most "homogeneous" of groups a wide range of individual expression is to be found (Hart 1954:242–261). As a fieldworker must learn to choose whom to trust and engage in certain endeavors, a teacher has to learn which of his children are most responsive in different classroom activities and subject areas. Gill was our mathematician; Donny our sportsman; Wilma our actress; Everett our writer; and Nancy our spokesman. Even where individual personalities had to be molded in certain ways, these alterations hinged on the creation of relevant conditions for change, not in undermining the usual perceptions children had of themselves. To be sure, the experience of anthropologists has been clearly that innumerable life styles exist as suitable adaptations to the demands and perceptions of human existence.

Education at Harlem School ought to have had as its major function the preparation of children for cultural worlds yet unknown, still to be fashioned. Reducing all to a central core and mode of expression would not necessarily equip them for life in a world constantly being reshaped. Because a child at Harlem School was unlikely to inherit his father's business, possessed no stock, did not change his clothing after school each day, might not celebrate his birthday with a party every year, and owned no wristwatch, does not mean he is not possessed of a large inventory of personal and social skills. Indeed, in class 6-4, children's descriptions of events and associations in their lives revealed their many capabilities.

FRANK

Since I was about 7 years old I began work around the house, such as washing dishes, sweeping the flore and going to the store. I did these things mostly because I asked. Sometimes my mother was not home to teach me so I had to learn myself. Then I began to like it some much that it became a habit finally a job. This job was like any other job only you didn't get paid for it. While doing my work if I did something wrong I would get yelled at, hit, or sometimes beaten. As I grew older I learned about things that you had to careful with such as matches, iorning and gas. A few years later I knew how to fold things like shirts very well, as the years went by the job became boring so gragarlly I lost some of my skills. Up till now I still do the same jobs but there are things added, baby-sitting.[7]

---

[7] This writing, and all that follows by the children, is edited in only a minor way to allow a reasonable flow in the meaning intended. Otherwise, these were uncorrected versions (spelling, grammar, and so forth) of the children's writing.

Frank continues in other writing, describing a typical day's activities.

> . . . I awoke at 7:30 A.M., woke my sister so she could go to school. My Mother left to work a littel earlyer than my father who left at 7:30.
> I left for school at 8:30 but first I took my brother over to the lady that mindes him. . . .
> At 3:00 P.M. played around with some girls with Larry. At 3:30 took clothing to the cleaner . . . . went back home and made a snack . . . fried some chicken for my mother as I was told. When my mother came home she finished making the food while I looked at T.V. After I saw the picture I went to get my brother and sister. For a half hour I was helping my mother while my brother and sister played. I sent my sister to bed, and gave my brother a bath, then I ate. After eating I washed the dishes, went to get the night paper, came back and . . . went to bed about 10:30.

Frank's experience ably shows the kind of skills he is required to use at home on a daily basis. Many have alleged that poor children are irresponsible and undependable in personal and household chores (Riessman 1962:41–43). But obviously this is not quite the case. The skill in ironing shirts and cooking is usually not developed until a much older age by more advantaged children, if at all. Other children in Project Class had similar skills. Though some children were defined by school people as "surly" and "cynical," they showed a deep sense of humor about themselves and others.

Everett

A day of my life

> My Mother drags me out of bed in the morning. I go in the bathroom wash up, eat my breakfast. Then I put on my coat and hat, and I'm off for school.
> In school I fool around till the teacher comes. Then I sharpen my pencil, do my work.
> At lunch time I eat my lunch, go to the park play some tag, then fight with class 6-1, come back to school instead of playing hookie. Try to sneak pass Miss S. but never succeed. Then get on line.
> After lunch come up stairs and fool around till teacher comes. Crack jokes, do my work sometimes, beat up Nancy and Wilma. Get on line when the teacher calls me, walk downstairs, chase Wilma home.
> At home take out my mutt, play some basketball, come up stairs and eat, then go to the center. Play some ping pong, go back home to watch T.V., eat. Then go to bed.
> And then I sleep happily ever after. After a hard day of play.

Everett, it will be recalled, is an outstanding student. And he was a child from a very poor family. When school conditions allowed, however, he was most humorous and energetic. As he reported it, in fact, he renamed his "mutt" from "Mutt" to "Sputnik" when the Soviet Union achieved its first space success in 1957.

Wilma also shows in her writing what a typical day is like in her life. She had an acute sense of the multifaceted aspects of her own personality. An astute observer of others, she was able to play a variety of roles as different social involvements required these.

Today is Thursday

7 O'clock, I'm still sleeping
8 O'clock, just awakening
9 O'clock, just dashed out the door.
10 O'clock, 11 O'clock, I'm in school
12 O'clock, Oh boy lunchtime
1 O'clock, just made it into the classroom
2 O'clock, 3 O'clock, school
4 O'clock, snoring back
5 O'clock, up and ready to go
6 O'clock, eating
7 O'clock, running from the boys
8 O'clock, just made it into the house to eat
9 O'clock, have to do that homework
10 O'clock, ran up to my friend's house
11 O'clock, banging on the door but nobody comes . . .
12 O'clock, Here comes someone
1 O'clock, eating
2 O'clock, getting ready to go to bed, have a fight with my sister. Mother half kills me. Ready for 40 winks.

This schedule, if indeed actual, reveals that Wilma spends most of the day on her own. Her mother worked a full shift in the evening. Thus, Wilma's education in the streets is significant in understanding her activities in school. Her remarkable ability to fulfill the roles required of her in school made her an outstanding student. She herself casually said that she was a "different" person on different occasions. "On Saturday I'm a real tomboy. On Sunday I'm a nice little girl. On holidays I'm everything. On school days I'm half tomboy and girl."

Donny's writing gave indication of his interests and the importance of peers and older boys in his life. He learned much about community life by hanging out with the fellows. It also gave him an "organizational sense" in that his different sports activities involved him in a variety of groupings. In class he was very adept at establishing orderly ways of getting things done. Playing games and establishing "work" crews was his responsibility. He often spoke about his "outside" contacts. These contacts made his real and imagined feats loom larger than they may have actually been.

DONNY

My Most Unforgettable Character

My most unforgettable character is Donoven Kearney. He taught me how to play basket ball. He mostly taught me how to shoot. I was always a good dribler. But he taught me how to follow the rules. I still don't always follow the rules but I do my best. That isn't all he did he even fixed my bike "free of charge". Every body was having a good time with their bikes except me. So Donoven came up to my house to see my big sister. And I asked him to fix my bike. So he fixed it. I went outside and had a good time with my bike. I played racing, tag, and just riding along until the police started to give out fines. I went upstairs so I couldn't get one. On my way up I got two flat tires. I told Donoven to fix it but he refused. He was with my sister and didn't want to be disterbed. He was my most unforgettable person. I will never forget Donoven Kearney. He is sixteen now and he is still my pal.

There is the suggestion in this writing that older boys effect important influences in younger children. They serve as cultural models for children's aspirations and anticipations as to whom they may later become. Similar to the way in which college students have assisted high school students in tutorial programs, it is quite possible that high school boys can be success-fully utilized to work with elementary school children. Not only Donny, but others in Project Class were influenced by older friends and relatives. They formed another cooperative unit by which cultural transmission took place. Again, the inclusion of neighborhood persons in learning endeavors for chil-dren would have been worth exploring. There well might have been some things young persons could convey that older people could not.

Peer group strength was evident among the girls too. This contradicted the thought that children at Harlem School could not get along with one another. The clique structure and solidity of the peer groupings in Project Class showed this not to be the case. Hortense, for example, wrote about Inez, whom she referred to as her "sister," or "blood sister."

HORTENSE

The person I can never forget is my sister. We play, dance, and go places with each other. We often where each others clothes and sometimes we have arguments, but after a while we stop fighting and make up to each other. She is short and sometimes we make fun of her and we have lots of fun. When I grow up I won't ever forget my sister. If I loose something she is always willing to help me find it. We share everything we have. I have only one wish for her that she can work harder in school so she can graduate this year she is in the 6th grade and is not doing so well in school. I try to help her but sometimes her work gets a little difcult for me to do. But if there's anything I can do to help her I would do it. She is my only sister and I love her. If anything ever happen to her I'd properly die from loveness. If only I could help her in her schooling. Because I want her to grow up and try to get a nice job in a big building somewhere downtown and I hope she make it.

Nancy similarly wrote about her friend Wilma. Nancy knew that Wilma was smart, but she felt herself more worldly about neighborhood goings-on; their relationship was a highly complementary one. Each was talkative and highly adaptable. In class there was little they could not accomplish together if they had a mind to do so. More interestingly, they knew quite well what their own abilities were. They had a recognizable confidence in themselves and one another.

NANCY

My best Friend

My best friend is Wilma. Why she is, because Wilma and I understand each other. I like her abilities, they are good. I like to talk with her, because I like to make her understand the things she didn't know. But once in a while we don't get along so good, because one of us are doing wrong to the other. But other times we are very close togather. When we have a problem we tell each other it. Wilma is very bright and interagent, and so am I. But sometimes we are very playful in school. We are ready to work also. We like to do our work sometimes ona typewriter. Wilma know her work. She work hard and study a lot. But I like Wilma a lot.

Nancy and Wilma liked to send me brief notes in class. One might read, "In your coat the showders are too broad" or "Your pants are too big." On occasion they would offer advice as to how we might proceed in class or how I was to discipline children: "Keep Everett in after school today." At still other times they told me I was "too soft," or they asked "if teachers work only for the money." Wilma, reflecting on teaching wrote, "I must say myself from the looks of things teaching is too hard, that's why I'll stick to my acting." Indeed both she and Nancy were acting often. They would have become fine teachers in later years, had they been inclined to want to teach.

Other children wrote about things personal to them alone. Some even attempted to make their own movie. Two reels of five minutes each were managed before they became caught up in the excitement of approaching graduation and dropped the project. Instead, they thought about their new school and what junior high school life would be like. And I wondered how their new aspirations would fit in with the old conditions of their existence. Would they see the world as more amenable to their desires? I thought about Donna's writing.

What I want to be When I Grow up

I want to be a housemaid to help people who need help. Like people who have over 5 children. I would help the old people. But I would help the people who need help most of all. Because I had a housemaid before and she help us out. So I would like to be a housemaid. I would be good to the children and their mother.

The press of poverty in the lives of the children was great, and they needed a confident vision that things were just not naturally so for them, that they would not always have to live in poverty because of who they were. So many of the children at Harlem School felt resigned to an inferior fate because the school held no alternative vision up to them. I hoped Project Class would understand that a substantive formal education might appear as one hope toward ameliorating the conditions under which poor people are forced to live.

PROJECT CLASS GRADUATES

The time eventually came at the end of my two years with Project Class when the children were to be graduated. The children had made it through four years and two teachers since the special program had begun for them in third grade. They were third-graders no longer. They had met the many challenges they had to confront. And each one had contributed to the evolution and shaping of the entire group. They were ready for the seventh grade. Unexpectedly for me there was talk by Harlem School officials about retaining Charlotte in the sixth grade, while the other children would be moved on to their new school. This time, however, I was so aroused that officials quickly dropped the thought. Not just Charlotte was involved; Norma had made Charlotte her special project and was proud of her accomplishments with her. I was not going to tolerate disappointment to either of them by allowing Charlotte to be held back.

Gill was virtually a young man by graduation time. He had become a true leader and a fine student. In fact much could be said about each of the children. I had now spent four years at Harlem School, and Project Class had given meaning and purpose to my life at the school. My feeling at their leaving was one of great loss. My emotional investment in them had been extensive. I really was concerned that I would not be able to reach commensurate feelings with subsequent groups of children. This was not to say that other children would be seen with less integrity or that they would not be treated as required. It meant that I knew Harlem School would never again provide the same kinds of external conditions and internal freedom that prevailed in Project Class. In any case I was not, still, an expert teacher, but I was, to be sure, very much a different person from the one I had been when I had come to the school originally. I had also acquired along the way the necessary credentials for being a regular, fully licensed teacher. However, I began to be interested in the training of teachers from the point of view of anthropology. At Harlem School it had been clearly revealed to me that it was difficult to revise teacher attitude and instructional technique once a teacher was on the job. One became a victim of the social system and took on the attributes perceived as required of his position in the system. Thus, teachers did not always find that they were driven in their tasks by the objective imperatives of teaching, but were motivated by personal and peripheral concerns (Little 1956:22–24). To have really excellent teachers of poor children, it seemed to me, deliberate and extensive pretraining programs were needed. Many children had suffered at the hands of teachers who were unequipped and unconcerned in their tasks. I still remembered my own compromising and inadequate efforts as a beginning teacher. It also was clear in my mind that schools in the slums would have to develop within the faculty "cadres of conscience" with regard to disadvantaged children. Too many teachers had prejudiced and ugly attitudes about children that went unchallenged by other teachers. These other teachers would have to speak up.

In the hope of keeping alive a sense of experimentation and a willingness to search for reasonable alternatives to traditionally employed ways, I asked for a first-grade class in my fifth year at Harlem School. I wondered if a man might have a different influence on early grade children. My request was denied by Mr. Green. He told me that regulations precluded such an assignment. "Young children are afraid of men," he told me. "Besides," he said, "what do you want the little ones for? You have to wipe their behinds all the time. It's a dirty job." Instead, he asked me to take a sixth-grade class of "underachievers." These were children with high IQs who did not attain full realization of their potential. I agreed to work with this group, and it proved to be a very interesting opportunity, even though it was really intended by school officials that this class be a "glorified Opportunity Class." The children were regarded as severe discipline problems, and this is why the class was given to me. In fact, the children easily attained grade levels in reading and subject fields in which they had an interest. They were not a "problem" at all. After five months another teacher was granted leave, and I was reassigned to a fourth-grade class. I was the first male teacher these children would have. It was the brightest class on the grade, and my adjustment to them consisted largely of granting outlet for their many extraordinary talents. By performance these children were the highest achievers I had taught. I was also pleased to find that two children in the class were sisters of children from Project Class. It kept me in contact with the parents of these children and informed me of the progress being made by them in junior high school.

In my next year at Harlem School I was again assigned an Opportunity Class, this time in the fourth grade. The same format for assigning children to classes continued to be employed by Harlem School officials. No significant or lasting educational innovations had really come to the school in my time there except for the Project Class program. It was true that the "Higher Horizons" program had been instituted, but it altered little at the school. Procedures in the classroom remained the same, despite a new program name. At midyear I left Harlem School. A major part of my own education had taken place in the five and one-half years I had spent there. It was an experience that was sure to influence all my subsequent activities, educational and personal.

11 / Disadvantage: some perspectives

IT IS AS FALSE to assume that one is necessarily prepared to teach after four years of teacher training in college as it is to assume that a man is prepared to kill after sixteen weeks of basic training in the military. I do not intend to equate the two activities of course. I mean, on the other hand, to indicate that my experience at Harlem School revealed to me that most teachers should, in fact, be doing something else. It is similarly false to assume that a teacher becomes intimate with each of the thirty or so children in his or her class, even over the span of a year. Few persons are intimate with any thirty people in their immediate lives. This is precisely what is happening in schools; teachers seek the rewards of their labors, not on the job, but in boat basins, through recreational activities in their private lives, and on the backyard lawns of their homes. For the children, however, school is a major portion of their personal lives, and the continued dissatisfaction placed on them precludes reward. They too are forced to seek reward elsewhere.

The education of children has been seen for too long as an intuitive process. Thus, when intuition fails, there is the tendency to label children as nonconforming, disruptive, and outside the mold we have artificially created for them. Yet one wonders if outspoken children do not keep alive for us the hope that we must alter our views and thereby assign new meaning and purpose to the transmission of culture in our schools. Their restlessness preserves for us the chance to overcome our centripetal attitudes about their capabilities for learning. As long as the pot boils someone has to look after it. The examination of Harlem School has revealed that the requirements for being a student were much more stringent than were the requirements for being a teacher. And the penalties for failure in the student role were much more harsh and longer lasting than the penalties for failing to teach. The teacher-learner relationship was not reciprocal; rather, it placed an altogether incommensurable burden on the child. It placed him at a disadvantage in the strivings toward reasonable life chances. Problems unsurmounted in the classroom made for compounded problems in later years, diminishing the skills with which his education purportedly prepared him.

Notably, the technological age deepens the problem of personal competence for minority members above all others. . . . Cultural and technical competence becomes a critical matter, and its threshold is raised as more education and more skill becomes essential for functioning adequately in society.

The lost young man in our time is the one who does not have a salable skill, or even the cultural know-how necessary to hawk products door-to-door, let alone to comprehend the social forces that shape his world and his life. . . . Defective education has a prolonged influence, particularly for minorities (B. Clark 1962:87).

One aspect of disadvantage, then, is to be denied the skills, knowledge, and attitudes required for fullest participation in our culture. It is as if in a hunting society one were denied the skills and temperament needed for the hunt even when survival depended on these. Or, for that matter, it would be as if one were adequately equipped for the hunt, but was then not permitted to hunt. "Any society selects some segment of the arc of possible human behaviour, and in so far as it achieves integration its institutions tend to further the expression of its selected segment and to inhibit opposite expressions. . . . To understand the behaviour of the individual . . . it is necessary . . . to relate his . . . responses to the behaviour that is singled out in the institutions of his culture" (Benedict 1959a:254). Failure to properly educate the individual results in his exclusion from the major institutional arrangements of his time. This exclusion further prevents him from learning the requisite behavior for his inclusion, thus precluding his chances in a tightening circle about him.

When one is miseducated and excluded, his legitimate claims on the culture remain unfulfilled. He finds himself without commitment to those forms of participation denied him. His fate, however, is in the hands of the economic, political, and religious forces that command his existence, forces that render him powerless in their influence on him. Disadvantaged persons are also those who, as a result, have relatively little control of the social influences on their own life—or the means by which to avoid them for that matter. Indeed, the poor are those who do not even have the wherewithal to get out of the way of the larger society's "beneficence." The many "poverty programs," allegedly in their behalf, are accorded them usually without choice. Harlem School offered an example of this quite clearly. Hundreds and hundreds of children emerged from its confines with educational aspirations unfulfilled, yet parents have been helpless in reversing this course toward repeated failures with children. School policy was not in their hands, but in the hands of others, whose own children did not have to attend Harlem School. Obviously, being disadvantaged is being constantly at the mercy or service of others.

Denial, exclusion, powerlessness, defenselessness, and lack of opportunity for fulfillment all contribute to personal loneliness and feelings of anxiety, a state of transition that seems ever to be so (Turnbull 1963). Those who are disadvantaged remain unincorporated in the associations needed to gain control over their own lives. The result of this may be distorted perceptions of self and perhaps skewed personality development. The individual becomes vulnerable in his encounters with others and wonders if their images of him are more correct than his own. This places a heavy burden on the person seeking relevant behavioral choices for himself. For some children in Harlem this was an imposition difficult to undo.

> One's hair was always being attacked with hard brushes and combs and Vaseline: it was shameful to have "nappy" hair. One's legs and arms and face were always being greased, so that one would not look "ashy" in the winter-time. One was always being mercilessly scrubbed and polished, as though in the hope that a stain could thus be washed away—I hazard that the Negro children of my generation, anyway, had an earlier and more painful acquaintance with soap than any other children anywhere. . . . Yet it was clear that none of this effort would release one from the stigma and danger of being a Negro; this merely increased the shame and rage. There was not, no matter where one turned, any acceptable image of oneself, no proof of one's existence. One had the choice, either of "acting just like a nigger" or of *not* acting just like a nigger—and only those who have tried it know how impossible it is to tell the difference (Baldwin 1963b:73).

At Harlem School the child had the choice of conforming to the images teachers held of him or of not conforming to them, which only increased their wrath. The choice was often not much of a choice. If the child would not be docile, he was called "defiant.". This form of negative definition of others is another characteristic of being disadvantaged. The falsely charac-terized, the misunderstood, and the disliked are all among the disadvantaged. For children this meant being precluded from having the wider choices of life style open to others. It meant being consigned to a particular style with-out opportunity to discriminate among other available standards. One's life is thus appropriated by unfamiliar cultural forces, or misappropriated as it were. Indeed it is well known that blacks live on an average seven years fewer than whites in America. This is directly attributable to being poor. This results in millions of years of life misappropriated. One wonders what could otherwise be done with these years of life. Being poor means living less. It was not impetuous to have asserted earlier that teachers are the caretakers of hundreds of lives.

In my judgment there has traditionally been a mix-up of values regarding the poor in our culture, particularly the nonwhite. For American Indians, who are in so many instances genuinely "culturally different," we have pursued a policy of forced detribalization against their will (Lesser 1961:1–9). For blacks, whose lives have been shaped by their American experience, we assert "difference" as if to lend a rationale for the prejudice and discrimination forced on them. For the rest of us we have reserved freedom of choice. And the schools have been instrumental in perpetuating these attitudes. If, for example, people are excluded from full participation in culture, there must be those who are willing to do the excluding. They are also products of our schools; and, if they do not learn those prejudices in school, it is even more clear that the school accomplishes little in being rid of them. Reshaping the lives of the disadvantaged certainly requires reshaping the lives and education of the advantaged. Neither group as presently constituted would exist if not for the other. It may well be that the disadvantaged child, by his nonaccept-ance of what is unacceptable, will eventually liberate the advantaged child as well.

The disadvantaged child has dared call attention to the Emperor's clothes by asking: "What's really in education for me?" In a counterpoint of innocence and defiance, the ghetto student declares that school is phony, that teachers don't talk like real people, that his reality as painted by the language of the school are as night and day.

In questioning whether the school has much intrinsic meaning, he has become the spokesman for the middle-class child as well (Fantini and Weinstein 1967:105).

Yet, some may think that schools housing more advantaged students are all right as they are. Still others, however, think not.

What educational institutions now do, in rough outline, is to take the child —warm, living flesh-and-spirit in the kindergarten and nursery school—and turn him into sinew, skeleton, scar tissue at the high school, college, or graduate school exit. He comes full of life and leaves full of schemes. He comes open and leaves closed. He comes in sensitive self-awareness and goes clad in armor. He comes singing, skipping, and dancing and leaves carrying himself, presenting himself, "using himself," posturing. He comes to give and receive; he leaves to trade at the door of life. Not out of some inherent necessity of "growing up"— indeed this is growing down—but out of the very structure and content of education designed to that end. And rightly so, for what we have needed hitherto were not human beings but skilled ants, and the institutions appropriate to their production, our schools and colleges, have been and are, mostly, ant hills (Seeley 1967:292–293).

But if "thinking, then, can be viewed as the purposeful definition of feeling,"[1] what feelings are children to derive in the school? Have we really given this the thought it merits?

We pride ourselves on the fact that we can make machines that think like human beings and overlook the fact that we have made millions of human beings who think like machines.

So that social change may be sound, so that human change will be sound, we need to teach the young how to think critically, creatively, originally, imaginatively, and daringly.

Indispensable as it is, the ability to think soundly is not enough. Man is not alone a thinking creature; he is also a feeling creature. Just as he has to be taught how to think, so, too, he has to be taught how to feel (Montagu 1966: 13–14).

It is easy for the teacher to like the "ideal" child: the one with the puffy cheeks, the close-cropped hair, who does his homework on time, raises his hand before he speaks, and goes to the bathroom only infrequently at school. But surely schools can accommodate children of more diverse persuasion as well. This would in no way undermine the teaching task; it could not be more abrasive than it now is. There are many things which give people satisfaction, passion, and a sense of power and accomplishment. And there are teachers who well know how to instill these feelings in children (Ashton-Warner 1963). But it requires a willingness to see the classroom as a place for the

---

[1] Mitchell (1967:39). The author outlines his concepts for world education, and the program instituted toward this end at Friends World Institute. The program is oriented toward the involvement of students in different culture areas of the world.

legitimate expression of emotion and thought, not as a place for their sup-
pression.

> I have never solved the "discipline problem," but I no longer believe it
> needs solution. Children will disagree with each other and with the teacher;
> they will be irrational at times, and the teacher will be, too. An atmosphere
> must exist in the classroom where conflict, disagreement, and irrationality are
> accepted temporary occurrences. No child, because he defies, should thereby
> have to become "a defiant child," or because he refuses to work, "a lazy child."
> Such labeling makes the classroom a harsh, unforgiving place, a world not fit for
> children or adults (Kohl 1967b:21).

This posture requires courage and the ability to withstand the criticism
of those who do not like departing from traditional ways of doing things.
However, such choices between failure and nerve must constantly be made
in the slum school (Henry 1966:14a). If the dentist continually left his
patients with a toothache or the doctor failed to heal, we would revise
our estimates of who they were and the tasks they purport to perform. As
in the case where a girl cannot cook, we might say she had been failed by
those whose responsibility it was to teach her this skill. In school as well
the child who has not learned has been failed by the persons whose job it
was to teach him. This is, in addition, a societal failure. "The pervasive
influence of teachers on our social structure must clearly be understood. . . .
It is the classroom teachers who exert the most significant influence upon the
short- and long-term social shape of our communities" (Wright 1967:74).

Being disadvantaged is also being blamed for who you are and being
punished for it. It might, for example, show itself in a second-grade class
with a teacher who is not really interested in children's feelings or in his or her
own lack of them.

> It seems to the observer that Mrs. Auslander is spending all her time pushing
> the children around, frequently hurting them as well. At the moment she is
> pinching Allen on the arm; he grimaces in pain. Then she shoves him to the
> corner. He begins to cry. Moments later similar events befall a boy named
> Edward.
> Suddenly, Mrs. Auslander makes an attempt at teaching the concept of time.
> "What time is it?" she calls out. A child begins to pack up his books and
> arranges his briefcase, perhaps taking her cue. But she turns to him sharply,
> "What time do you go home? Put your books down. It's not time to go home."
> She notices that Carol has left the corner and joined a group that is back
> lingering near the observer. "So you want me to smack you. Get back in the
> corner and put your hands on your head." Carol does so and starts sucking
> her thumb again. . . .
> Things seem to be getting worse. . . .
> The teacher pulls a child by the hair. It is kinky short hair on a Negro boy's
> scalp. It hurts, and he yells (Moore 1964:88–89).

Disadvantage also means that you are seen as having few personal rights.
And it means that you get angry and refuse to accept the unwarranted dis-
affection of others. It means exploding inside when there is no outlet for
your aroused feelings, and it means exploding outwardly when this is neces-

sary so that you might maintain some minimal semblance of your positive perception of yourself.

> Now, I admit, a teacher has hit me before, but a teacher never got away with it. When a teacher hit me before, he said, "_____, get that hat off." I told him, "You say please before I do anything for you." This teacher was constantly riding my back, a teacher named Mr. _____, he was a white teacher. I . . . I didn't know nothing about their prejudice at that time and I was in that school. . . . He told me, I was walking through the building, you know, it was time to go home so I just put my hat on because I had some books in my hands, you know, and I was fixing them together—he said, "_____, take your hat off." I said, "You say please." He said, "Who the hell are you asking to say please to you? I'm a teacher, you don't ask me to say please to you—I'm your superior." I said, "Is you jiving, man?" I said . . . I walked away from him and he grabbed me on my coat. I said, "Okay, I'll take my hat off." He said, "No," he said. "You a wise guy," he said, "you a wise guy, huh? You one of them black wise guys, huh?" I said, "You got some nerve, calling me black," I said. "Okay, I'll pass off here, let me go and I'll go on home about my business and I'll forget this ever happened." He said, "No, you a wise one. Come on in here." He took his keys out like, he took his glasses off and put them in his pocket, he took his watch off and put it on the table when he got in the room, he closed the room and the door was locked on the outside. He take his jacket off and uncuff his sleeves and roll them up. I look at him and I was standing there laughing. He walks up to me and he hit me in the face with a right hand—he smacked me into the stars. I dropped my books. My mouth flew open wide, I was shocked, surprised, this teacher hitting me. That teacher in that room, they had to come in there and get me off that teacher. It took four of them to come and get me off that teacher (Fuchs 1965:90–91).

For the children at Harlem School disadvantage meant learning for the first time that there is something about some white people that you did not know before. They were distant and mechanical in response. Some even seemed hateful. As a young child you might wonder if there is something wrong with you. Why are you scorned and disapproved? School becomes a place where teachers tell you to "shut those thick lips" and to "behave like a human being." And small events are impressed on your mind forever, just as others have experienced these—for example, the poem "Incident":

> Once riding in Old Baltimore
>   Heart-filled, head-filled with glee,
> I saw a Baltimorean
>   Keep looking straight at me.
>
> Now I was eight and very small,
>   And he was no whit bigger,
> And so I smiled, but he poked out
>   His tongue, and called me, "Nigger."
>
> I saw the whole of Baltimore
>   From May until December;
> Of all the things that happened there
>   That's all that I remember.
>
>   (Cullen 1947:9)

It is difficult to calculate the impact on the person of such events, but it is clear that they do not serve to foster friendship and intercultural understanding (Coles 1964). The education of children at Harlem School seemed more like bottling soda, an assembly line procedure where the cap is put on each child, whether it fits or not. Few teachers were sincerely able to build a commitment to such a task when they were able to examine it for what it was.

THE MULTIFACETED ROLE OF TEACHERS

To handicap a child mentally is as if to handicap an animal organically. Man's response to his environment is cultural and skewed perceptions alter the course of one's natural history in all subsequent events. One would not tie down a seal's flippers and expect him to swim. Neither can we fail to educate the children of poor people and then expect them to derive the full benefits of our culture. Just as poverty is a leading cause of physical death (*The New York Times* 1964:59), miseducation is a leading cause of intellectual death.[2] The teaching task in the slum school needs to be redefined and expanded. And the focus has to be on that task, not on the child or his alleged inabilities. I suspect very strongly that were poor children made rich somehow we would not be concerned with "how they think" or if they are "culturally different." These preoccupations have been by-products of our failure to look to the core of educational practice and to see it as it really is, perhaps in this case through the child's eyes. This much is certain: teachers cannot pretend to address themselves to the solutions of black children's problems before they come to grips with the very formidable problems they themselves face at the parental generation level. It is here that race prejudice and ethnic separation have their roots. A teacher who has not seen it relevant in his own life to have black friends cannot really be a friend to black children, that some people have fashionably learned to say "black" instead of "Negro" notwithstanding. Cultures are forged by adults not by children, and the resolution of educational and social problems must come from them.

There is great need for revision in teacher training programs—for all teachers and certainly for teachers who will be working with poor children. Needed in such training is the inclusion of socially productive community work: in welfare agencies, hospitals, and other places where there is opportunity to come together with those we have up to now considered "them." Practice teaching has virtually been the sole interpersonal involvement the teacher trainee gets. But even here the focus has been the child exclusively. There has been little emphasis on the process of cultural transmission.

---

[2] See Hentoff (1966). The author cites the efforts of one courageous New York City administrator to prevent children from "dying" in the schools. The battle, nevertheless, is a most difficult one.

> In the many discussions of urban education for the new child of the slum, little attention is given to the interactional setting within which it is to occur and the possible influences of this social environment on the educational function of the school. On the contrary it is usually taken for granted that the traditional order of relationships within the school and between the school and the slum neighborhood will not be the object of change but that the problem is to prepare the child for school or to provide ways and means of helping him adjust to formal schooling. Yet the present structure of the school in the slum neighborhood is one which all too often is conducive to the custodial care of the child rather than his education and to the establishment of the school as an enclave viewed with fear or even hostility by both parent and child (Eddy 1967:169–170).

Teachers need the opportunity to see those unfamiliar to them in positions of worth and esteem. This comes only by relevant involvements in social groupings that permit new values to emerge and take hold. Certainly the inclusion of such experiences in teacher training programs would be as important as participation in intramural sports, fraternities, ROTC, gym, and the host of other activities that adorn college life. Perhaps in this way the teacher can see a more extended commitment for himself beyond the classroom to the larger society.

Teaching at Harlem School and places like it cannot be viewed as charity work or the temporary tranquilization of children. Our allusions to children's incapacities are really illusions about ourselves. And the management theory that undergirds activity at Harlem School has to be replaced by needed theories of change and culture, which, in turn, will give rise to more adequate theories of learning. The teacher clearly has a multifaceted role. There is the teaching role: arranging the classroom for learning by the appropriate use of space, materials, and children; conveying subject matter in terms and styles representative of that subject matter; and lending the encouragement and example necessary to be supportive of children's efforts.

There is the academic role of teachers which requires constant schooling and retooling in subject matter, the meaning of change to be understood, and the constant awareness of the culture concept as it relates to all things all persons do. It also means revealing the spirit and image of particular disciplines to oneself, to understand the ethical imperatives of various sciences. Finally the academic role implies a willingness to search for adaptable models for instruction that will replace intuition and whim as the basis for deciding how to proceed in the classroom (Bruner 1960).

There is the research role of teachers too. It requires the systematic investigation of the nature of classroom grouping, the nature of children's creativity, and the search for values in instruction. For example, we are fairly successful at getting boys to be boys as it were, and girls to behave as we think females ought to. We know this is learned behavior. Why can't we get children, if not to love one another, at least to appreciate cultural and behavioral diversity? It is my judgment that these values can be successfully taught if they were given priority as other things—clean fingernails and such—are presently given priority. Up to now little research has come out of the schools. Teachers clamor for more appropriate techniques of instruction but have not themselves developed many. With so many school districts throughout the country one would think that some meaningful research would come out of the schools each year, yet it really does not. Teachers are, after all, best situated to see how children succeed or fail (Holt 1965).

An additional role for the teacher is the political role in shaping school policy. Here, there is a responsibility to help formulate more appropriate procedures for teacher certification and selection. There is the need to welcome and involve community representatives and parents in school affairs. There is also the need to restructure curriculum and choices of learning materials. For the most part, teachers at Harlem School did not even have a say in the books chosen as texts. Just as often they were unaware of the recently developed materials for classroom use; perhaps it was felt that this was not necessary toward maintaining oneself on the job. Indeed, a teacher's license is easier to keep than a driver's license.

With all this there is the need for a social, or reform, role among teachers. Though teachers do not normally live in the communities in which they teach, they have a responsibility toward helping to mold a viable community life style in a manner preferred by members of that community. Teachers know better than anyone else, except children's parents, what disadvantage means for children. For it is they who spend more time with poor children than others when children are not in the home. Poverty, however, cannot be seen by teachers as a problem only during school hours. Commitments must extend to the larger society to be real. Labor organizations speak for the worker and the church speaks for our religious preferences. The teacher likewise must speak for the total welfare of the child. Aloofness is complicity not "professionalism."

There is a great need for ethnographies on our schools. Though compulsory education is so central to our existence, few see it as something more than to be taken for granted. Fewer still are aware in depth of what happens to children in schools. There are innumerable themes to be inquired into; recruitment of teachers, student strategies in response to teachers, out-of-school learnings as they relate to in-school activities, peer group involvements, the teaching of values, the exceptional child, and the discrepancy between real and ideal culture. Others would include reference to the spatial and temporal dimensions of learning, the influence of the classroom culture system on the teacher, and the relationship of school to community. Deliberate study of these would reveal new insights into the relationship between the individual and his culture. Are there educational culture areas, for example? Certainly there appears to be a remarkable similarity among schools for children of the poor. Is the uniformity due to the alleged singular behavioral styles of the children or to the inflexible attitudes and practices of people who rule in such schools? School people must begin to ask questions. Palliative programs have not been a worthy substitute for real knowledge of our schools and the willingness to act on that knowledge.

I am inclined to view many of the programs and projects for the culturally deprived as another hula-hoop phase in which parlor liberals gain publicity for their beneficent undertakings. I am questioning, basically, whether these people have an intellectualized commitment to such programs, or whether the programs just happen to be their momentary effort at charity. It is tempting to equate most projects for the culturally deprived with the types of movements that come at Christmastime: primarily visceral as opposed to rational. It is "good" to give food baskets to the needy, and because "good" is intended no one need be overly concerned with the possible consequences of such action (Austin 1965:67).

But more than token concern for the education of the poor child is required. It is the whole shape of our culture that is in question.

We stand today in a crowded place, where millions of men mill about seeking to go in different directions. It is most uncertain whether the educational invention made by those who emphasized teaching or the educational invention made by those who emphasized learning will survive. But the more rapidly we can erase from our society those discrepancies in position and privilege which tend to perpetuate and strengthen the power and manipulative aspects of education, the more hope we may have that that other invention—the use of education for unknown ends which shall exalt man above his present stature—may survive.[3]

SUBURBAN POSTSCRIPT

Considerable emphasis has been given recently to the problems found in inner city schools. Relatively little attention has been paid to suburban schools, yet many of the same problems are to be found there. Increasing numbers of poor people now live tucked away in suburban enclaves, even more removed from sight than others among the poor. Most people like to think of the suburbs as places where children attend ranch-style schools where they reap the benefits of adequately tax-supported programs. In some instances this may be the case. But for many the same failure syndromes, accompanied by the same mythologies, are to be found. The same patterns of de facto segregation have been recreated. Instead of hearing "shut those thick lips," one can hear questions like the following: "Hey, do you know where I can get a couple of 'six-foot five' niggers for the basketball team? These colored guys can really jump." Many of the teachers who had "escaped" the inner city are now in the suburbs. Some have found themselves again teaching minority group children, and they resent it. They consider it an encroachment on exclusive territory. "These people are everywhere," they say. These teachers are among the most intractable in their dealings with disadvantaged children. They find great freedom from restraint in that few community organizations in the suburbs are potent in behalf of the poor. The lack of "ethnic mix" in some classes suggests to already prejudiced

---

[3] Mead (1964:174). This material is from "Our Educational Emphasis in Primitive Prospective," a selection in Dr. Mead's compiled writings.

teachers that the minority child is an "oddity." Even in the suburban university there is relatively little opportunity for white students to sit alongside blacks or Puerto Ricans. Teachers trained at such institutions come away with a great latent bias about nonwhite children because they have had no contact with them. They too fall victim to existing school mythologies. There are many students who have been to Rome, Paris, and Tel Aviv, but not to Harlem or Bedford-Stuyvesant. I have seen the results of this provincial training for teachers in suburban schools housing the poor. Culture shock and distorted perceptions, as in Harlem, are evident. The following description is of a first-grade class in a suburban "ghetto." Almost all the children in the class were black.

> The teacher trainee (student teacher) is attempting to teach "rhyming." It is early afternoon. Even before she can get the first "match" (for example, "book" and "look") a whole series of events is drawn out.
> One child plays with the head of a doll, which has broken off from the doll, alternately hitting it and kissing it.
> The student teacher tells a boy who has left his seat that he is staying-in after school. He begins to cry. Another child teases that his mother will be worried about him if he stays in after school. The boy now cries even harder and screams at the teacher: "You can't keep me in until 15 o'clock."
> A girl tries to answer a question put to the class but raises her hand with her shoe in it. She is told to put her hand down and to put her shoe on.
> Another child keeps switching his pencil from one nostril to another, trying to see if it will remain in his nose if he lets go of it; he is apparently wholly unconcerned with the session in progress.
> One child is lying down across his desk, pretending to sleep while seeing if the teacher sees him. Just next to him another child leads an imaginary band. Still a different child, on his other side, stands quietly beside his seat, apparently tired of sitting.
> While this is all going on the regular teacher of the class is out of the room. When she does return, she makes no effort to assist, or criticize, the student teacher. The student teacher later informed me that the regular teacher was not "just being polite." She rarely directed the student teacher, but simply let her "take over" the class on occasion. The student teacher also remarked that things were no different in the class when the regular teacher held forth.
> Fifteen minutes had gone by, but little "rhyming" had been accomplished. A boy begins to shadow box in the back; another talks to himself in acting out a scene he envisions.
> Still another child shakes his fist at the student teacher, mimicking her words: "cat-fat, hop-stop."
> Two children turn to each other and exchange "burns" on one another's forearms, while another child arranges and rearranges his desk materials and notebook, seemingly dissatisfied with each succeeding arrangement.
> A girl in the back has an empty bag of potato chips but is trying to use her fingers as a "blotter" to get at the remnants. She pretends to be paying attention to the lesson.
> Another child asks to go to the bathroom, but is denied.
> After a half-hour I left.[4]

---

[4] This school visit was in spring, 1965. Many visits have been made to many schools in the suburbs where similar patterns as described are drawn out. Some school districts have begun to hold in-service programs for teachers to better equip them for working with minority group children.

I was later told that the class I observed is "typical" for the grade. There is nothing wrong with the children; they are from poor families and "not much is expected from them." It was another instance of the early stages of failure for the children. By second grade they may be put on a "lower track" because they are "slow learners." Thus, their public schooling is patterned for them at age six or seven. By high school they may well be among the "pushouts," those we usually call the dropouts. The student teacher confessed readily that her preparatory work at college was of little consequence in having her understand the children. She knew nothing at all about the neighborhood from which the children came. She knew only that she "did not want to work with 'these' children when she became a regular teacher," although she "could probably get a job in this school."

Older children of the poor, except those who have been rendered docile and fearful, are more vocal in their objection to bad teaching. Perhaps they have been influenced by the social reordering taking place in our nation and the fact that many are eligible for the military and would prefer to stay in school instead. They are influenced as well by the civil rights movement and the general upheavals taking place on many university campuses. In working with a group of "Upward Bound" teenagers, I saw this "new" attitude quite clearly. These young people were students of higher potential than their school records indicated. The program was to encourage them to finish high school and perhaps go on to college if their school achievement qualified them. Many of the nonwhite students were unwilling to accept the usual negative definition of them given by their teachers in the public school. In the setting of the university where we worked with them, they were free and assertive in their attitudes. It was curious to note that in the attempt to formulate positive perceptions of themselves many had accepted some of the myths alleged in their behalf, but had "turned them around" as positive. For example, one black student in a session on anthropology asserted that blacks are innately better athletes than whites. I wanted, of course, to indicate that success in sports is mostly a matter of opportunity to exercise talent and not strictly a result of inherent qualities. We were drawn into debate about it.

> Teacher: "What do you mean blacks are better athletes than whites?"
> Student: "Well, look around. Who are the best guys?"
> Teacher: "Okay. Who you got in baseball?"
> Answer: "Mays, Hank Aaron, Bob Gibson."
> Teacher: "Football?"
> Answer: "Sayers, Adderly, Jimmy Brown."
> Teacher: "In basketball?"
> Answer: "Chamberlain, Bill Russell, 'Big O.' "
> Teacher: "How about tennis?"
> Answer: "Arthur Ashe." [Then there was a pause.]
> Teacher: "Who else?"
> Answer: "That's all we need, baby."[5]

[5] This exchange took place at a suburban university during the summer of 1967. These same students later attended a class in cultural anthropology in which I was the instructor during fall, 1967. Their willingness to see people in alternative light made them receptive to the "attitude" of anthropology, and they were excellent students.

Applause followed the last answer. It was clear that the black students in the class were unwilling to accept any image of black people as inferior. We went on to discuss the "scientific" fallacies in their thinking, and they submitted later that no ethnic or "racial" group has a priority on excellence, but that some people have attained heights in certain endeavors in which they received ample opportunity to develop their skills. When some persons of different minority groups did not gain prominence in certain activities, it was frequently noted that they had been excluded from participation in these activities. I was struck, however, by the more assertive behavior of the teenagers and the search for confidence in themselves. This too was derived from the mood and movement of the larger culture. The excluded are seeking to disengage themselves from the disadvantage our culture has imposed on them. They will not be content until the mission they see for themselves is accomplished. Indeed the university has a role to play in this mission. Many more members of nonwhite minority groups have to be admitted to college programs than have been up to now. Even the very young are infused with more purposive and militant attitudes. Harlem School and places like it will have to realize this and join in the forces now marshaling. The wise teacher will see that his own personal freedom is involved in his willingness to act in behalf of the poor child. As the child gets older he is less likely to be willing to wait himself.

> What, from the slums
> Where they have hemmed you,
> What, from the tiny huts
> They could not keep from you—
> What reaches them
> Making them ill at ease, fearful?
> Today they shout prohibitions at you
> "Thou shall not this"
> "Thou shall not that"
> "Reserved for whites only"
> You laugh.
> One thing they cannot prohibit—
> The strong men . . . coming on
> The strong men gittin' stronger
> Strong men . . .
> Stronger . . .
>
> (S. Brown 1962:14)

12 / The failure of slum school education: a reiteration

THE SEPARATION of black and white America is played out dramatically in the Harlem slum school. The disparity in educational attainment between black children of the poor and more advantaged children in other schools is in fact a primary cause of this separation. In Harlem School itself the gulf between teachers and children is an ever-widening one. I had returned to Harlem School to visit a year after I had left and was told by the principal that learning and discipline problems were "worse than ever." This was the case, despite the fact that school population had been reduced by one-third with the "open enrollment" plan and the shift of students to other schools. Obviously then, the problems of better education for Harlem children cannot be reduced to problems of class size or the physical plant. The failure of education in Harlem is the failure of cultural transmission; largely, the transmitting agency is to blame. It can only more fully explicate its role by a reassessment of the entire educational enterprise in the school. Neglect in so doing will only result in a greater proliferation of myths about children and a greater disenchantment of teachers for the job they have to perform.

There are larger implications, to be sure. The extent of one's formal education—and the quality of that education—is directly related to being poor. Poverty is a partial result of undereducation, and it is the poor who so often are afforded little chance in the schools. The cycle of diminished life's chances is reinforced in this way. The poor and miseducated have a much more certain chance of being underemployed, falling ill more often, living fewer years, and being buried in wayward marshland. They will also have a diminished commitment to a way of life that promises them anything but what they really need. The dissociation from the larger society sooner or later leads to dislike for that society. It has led in this country to a pervasive racism that infects teaching and what we teach, not only whom we teach. Whites and blacks feel their whiteness and blackness more personally as the gulf between them widens, and there is a tendency to attribute one's fate to these designations. The child who acts out in Harlem School serves as a premonition of the more overt demonstrations of discontent manifested in places we know as Watts, Newark, Detroit, and Washington, D.C. The beginning upheavals in suburban areas are a further extension of our educational neglect. Those who riot and those who put down riots are all products of our school systems. Quite obviously they do not all emerge from the process of schooling with the same attitudes and beliefs nor with strong loyalties to each other. If education has a different meaning for the disadvantaged person, it is because education has been indeed different for him. This does not mean that the more advantaged person has necessarily had the kind of education he needed, for the advantaged have permitted the disadvantaged to exist. This seems to me to be a gross educational shortcoming as well. If it is true that many blacks spend hours each day reminded of the meaning of what it means to be black in America, it ought to be that white persons spend a commensurate period each day thinking about the same thing. Then the meaning of being white would be clarified for the rest of us who are white. Though the teachers at Harlem School often felt their whiteness acutely, they were unaware of the racial feelings conveyed to children. The roots of failure ran deep at Harlem School and attitudes of teachers fed this failure.

TEACHER TRAINING AND SELECTION

It is difficult to select from the total cultural configuration where the failure of slum school education has its beginnings. It is no doubt true, however, that our present teacher training programs are oriented toward the technical and the psychological rather than to the cultural. Certification as an elementary schoolteacher in New York State does not require that a candidate have formal coursework in anthropology or community study. Educational methods courses predominate; thus, the elementary teacher is to be a generalist in a variety of subject matters without necessarily having to take into account family patterns, neighborhood settlement and dispersal arrangement, or the cultural factors influencing perception and behavior. These omissions in one's training render the teacher anxious and imperceptive of the ways and feelings of children. The behavior of the children is seen as "foreign" and improper in the school, prompting the teacher to seek mythical and imagined causes for his inability to more successfully communicate to them.

As my own instance has borne out, the testing and selection of teachers also leaves much wanting. Attention is paid to speech patterns and the like over and above the social and personal commitment and knowledge the teacher ought to be able to bring to bear in working with children. The proper articulation of "sixty-six sixty-sevenths" looms more important than the necessary personal imperatives of wanting to teach children of the poor. Quite clearly, very little up to now has been done to build into testing procedures a testing of the person's will to teach and the consequent necessity to involve oneself beyond the classroom in order that more suitable conditions for educating children be created. We have apparently been unable, or unwilling, to find alternative positions in the school for children who do not achieve, so that they might still function with integrity and status. Instead, we continue to have a variety of designations for "discarded" children by which we hide our callous disregard for them: Opportunity Class, G-track, Achievement Class, and Able Class are some of the mixed metaphors of educational procedure. At Harlem School, Opportunity Class meant almost complete absence of opportunity; it meant assignment to an educational junk heap. In the parental generation it is followed in many cases by the necessity to be on welfare and the personal feelings of doom which accrue when one is not educated for opportunity in employment or social mobility.

The assignment of teachers to classes is likewise a haphazard process. At Harlem School the "worst" and least experienced teachers were assigned to classes needing the most able and understanding teachers available. The result was that children were mistreated and miseducated, and the sincere beginner was disenchanted with the job because he could not find support and direction from other school people. The starting teacher puzzles over why he was not better prepared in his training and why school administrators are willing to diminish the chances for success with children at the very beginning of his career. More often than not, he finds few answers to his queries. He finds he must rely largely on himself. When he fails with children, his gloom, he finds, may be overcome by seeking the reasons for his failure in the children themselves. This seems fitting to him because all those around him have prepared him for this fantasy by their own behavior—teachers, principal, guidance counselors, and the rest. He begins to yearn for another place which would seem to him more congenial, or he strives to get out of the classroom, to be a guidance counselor or other specialist. For so many this is seen as the ultimate reward of a teaching career. And this is what is happening in so many college classrooms attended by teachers. They are working to acquire the credentials that will qualify them for attaining positions in education that will remove them from direct contact with children. Already exiled from his original intentions for teaching, the disgruntled teacher feels he will change his job since he cannot change the children.

Most teachers at Harlem School were ambivalent about their roles. They knew there were other factors involved in children's underachievement. There was the poverty of the children and the vacuousness of the school. It was a seesaw battle for many teachers who wanted to do more but found they did less. Mild forms of culture shock resulted in verbal denigration of the children or corporal punishment, which was too frequent. The children, in turn, responded with their own strategies, confirming for many teachers the negative appraisal they had at the start. When it was found by teachers that administrators at the school also showed disdain for the children, there was a joining of forces against the children. No one spoke for the child at all.

THE SCHOOL SOCIAL SYSTEM

No formal initiation or induction process existed for the new teacher at Harlem School. Ostensibly, student teaching while in college was to serve as the beginning of the rite of passage that was to move the person eventually to the status of full-fledged teacher. Yet, many had begun their teaching without the benefit of student teaching, and those who did have practice teaching as part of their training experienced this in schools very much different from Harlem School. Most often this was accomplished in a public school that had a relationship of some kind to the university attended by the student teacher. Once at Harlem School the teacher finds that prior experience does not jibe with the requirements made of him in the new place. He finds also that he was hired to fit a slot in the social system and not necessarily to seek his own personal and intellectual expression. Furthermore, the new teacher may not have taught black children before and more than likely he himself had never had a black teacher in his own educational experience. He, therefore, may never have had opportunity to see black people in positions of worth and power in his own relationships. And it is hard for him to imagine the children in his classes being distributed in the larger society in positions of worth when their education is completed. He has small vision of what his children may become in later life, for he has an even smaller vision of who they are at the present.

As he becomes adjusted to the job, the teacher begins to discern the social structure of the school. He finds that an underlying ethos pervades the slum school which prescribes and accepts failure for the child. Assistant principals function not as experts on curriculum and instruction, but as stock boys and disciplinarians. Boxes are constantly being unpacked and children are being reprimanded and punished. The principal seems more concerned with maintaining a stable staff, irrespective of its quality at times, than with effecting formidable school-community ties and fashioning relevant learning programs. Education appears as a process where children are merely the by-products, not the core of concern. Guidance counselors and reading specialists are preoccupied with norms and averages, not with the enhancement of learning for all the children. Theirs is a remedial task, and where one would not exist, they create it. School directives and bulletins are concerned with bathroom regulations and procedures along stairways, the worth of the children being assessed in terms of their ability to conform to these peripheral demands.

The new teacher at Harlem School learns that various teacher "types" emerge within the social system. Personal commitment and philosophy become ordered around the system, so that teachers vie for the "better" classes and the more pleasantly situated rooms. All want classes free of discipline problems, more equipment, and more free time. The clique structure among teachers forces the newcomer to choose a "teacher type" for himself; if he does not do so, he must be willing to seek his reward in independence from the others. He finds other new teachers who express the same dismay as he does. By contrast, there are the "old-timers" who seem to be doing things in the way that they were done ten and fifteen years before. The few black teachers on the staff apparently share no permanent or continuing relationship with white teachers after the school day, and the newcomer wonders what the black teachers think about their life at the school. He wonders how many of them are just as detached as most white teachers from the needs and feelings of the children. There are also the few teachers who seem to enjoy brutalizing the children, the ones who report with glee how they punish and discipline their children. There are also the routinized who are concerned with hanging coats on designated hooks and not with children's self perceptions. One finds the young women who will soon leave Harlem School for marriage or motherhood and the young men who hold second jobs in order to make financial ends meet, sometimes pouring more energy and personal investment into those other jobs. And there are the outright bigots who deny the worth and humanity of the children they teach and seize every opportunity to stifle and undermine them. One also perceives the teachers who seem oblivious to what is going on about them and seem overwhelmed by the task they face in teaching children, unaware of their own ineptitude. And finally the new teacher to Harlem School may see the "phony," the teacher who exudes love and lets children kiss her on the cheek at dismissal time as parents look on, but lives without love in the classroom and rules autocratically in subduing children's meaningful thoughts when no one looks on. It should be said as well that the new teacher will find the dedicated teacher too, the one who earnestly devotes his energy and spirit to educating the children and instilling a sense of hope and pride. But he is not found frequently and almost never in a position of power. This teacher knows well that he will be considered "radical" and "unusual" in acting this way—an odd-ball in the system. Yet for such a person, conscience and conviction survive.

Among these types, the beginning teacher finds it difficult to tell where he must fit into the system. He turns more and more inward, deciding he will preoccupy himself with his own class. He knows that even the clerical staff wields more power than he, deciding where equipment is placed and indeed, even where teachers and children are assigned. The various perfunctory duties one must perform add to the disillusionment and one searches for some form of inner strength to avoid succumbing to it all.

THE CLASSROOM CULTURE SYSTEM

Turning to the children, the new teacher sees the results of years of educational disenchantment. In the middle grades and beyond, children are already two or more years in arrears in academic achievement. Not knowing to what this is attributable, the teacher seeks an explanation. He wonders how you teach for what should have been two years before in the child's life. How do you eradicate the belief that Harlem School is an oppressive place, which is meaningless in your real life as a child? He realizes that children in class have developed counter-strategies in meeting teachers' aggressions and that they cannot tell at the outset whether a new teacher is to be believed or trusted. Most black adults have found it hard to accept the articulations of the white majority and the children bring the same warranted suspicions to school with them.

Yet, as he becomes more immersed in his own classroom, the teacher finds a wide variety of type and temperament among the children. The range in physical appearance alone evokes his enthusiasm. Children are alert and active, but sometimes subdued and detached as well. One is not certain which of the attributes possessed by children are more indicative than others, nor can he tell the covert aspects of the children's personalities. No overt characteristics tell the teacher precisely who each child is, despite the ease in which one selects these overt characteristics. One has to probe and to hold judgments as only tentative. Indeed, one wishes he had help. Because his presentations of subject matter are not always internalized readily by the children, the teacher finds that his inability to convey content leads to restlessness and interest in other things among them. If he is inclined to seek blame in others, he will conclude that bad discipline among the children is the cause for classroom failure. Once he crosses this mental divide, he becomes susceptible to the acceptance of a great encyclopedia of myths about children.

At Harlem School a vast array of myths about poor children is brought forth to allay the concern for their underachievement and miseducation. There is mention of deprivation, broken families, and the whole philosophic syndrome about poverty and underprivilege. But there is nothing philosophic or theoretical about being hungry or falling frequently ill; there is no need for the teacher to first conceptualize the problems his children face. The majority of teachers use the excuse of "not knowing enough" about the causes of poverty or of "not being responsible for what happened in the past." These are philosophies of postponement and avoidance of obligation, but they do not, in any case, ease the teachers' burden or the children's desperation in the classroom. The manifest symbols of poverty are played out in the classroom every day. The teacher knows that his failure with children will ensure their chances for being poor in later life, yet the teacher wonders what formal means exist for involvement in neighborhood and community. There seem to be no joint social structures for teachers and parents to combine efforts. It is easy to blame the absence of such structures on the "apathy" of parents and their "defiance" of school efforts.

The children too are seen as defiant and unconcerned, as if only in school to make the teacher's job more difficult. As a result the varying learning styles of the children are overlooked and bypassed in administering to them in the classroom. No connection is sought by the teacher among learning styles, classroom spatial and physical pattern, curriculum content, materials available, and the temporal context. Nor does the teacher come to realize that the maintenance of maximal learning conditions hinges on the interweaving of different temperamental and personality types. The social organizational pattern among the children must be perceived and worked with to utilize the creative strengths among the children in interaction. And the children's beliefs—their "world view"—must be seen alongside the often contrary beliefs and premises which undergird the behavior of the teacher and other school officials.

What happens to those involved in such a setting? Too frequently the result is rejection by teachers and children of one another. Each side may adopt severe methods against the other. Children will "play hooky" and withdraw from teachers' efforts. And teachers will make discipline the major subject matter, as it were, in the class. Lack of success in teaching prompts one at least to demand order in the classroom. If children cannot properly be taught, this failure must be kept unobtrusive. Management of the children's failure is thus resolved by discipline techniques. Mechanical tasks gain prominence and feelings are submerged. The caretaking function supersedes the transmission of culture function. And the teacher's safeguard becomes his anonymity. If one does not get involved, he need not build a commitment to what he does not get involved in. Anonymity precludes commitment. To work actively toward the improvement of school-community relations would take away one's anonymity; few are willing to risk this. Their facelessness preserves their privacy in the public world. But in the long run the teacher has to make himself known; he must post his philosophy alongside his room number. For many it is not easy to do this.

NEIGHBORHOOD AND SCHOOL

Though Harlem School belonged to the neighborhood, it was not psychologically a part of it. On the contrary, teachers felt unwanted, estranged. Perhaps this was why few ventured off the "beaten paths" to the "hinterland" beyond the school, into the side streets and the homes where the children played out their lives. Some teachers at Harlem School had never been to a single child's household, despite the fact that they had been employed at the school for many years. Nothing was known of community self-descriptions, the activity and social calendar in the neighborhood, the focal points for assembly and dispersal, or the feelings of residents toward the "outside world." Teachers could not imagine that they could foster a genuine coming-together of neighborhood persons and themselves. They hid behind their "professionalism." They failed to realize that the apathy and disparagement they associated with parents were attributed by the latter to them. It is not to be underestimated how "foreign" teachers feel themselves to be at Harlem School, how disliked by the children. Why then do they remain on the job? Part of the answer is in the fact that the rewards of one's work are not always sought on the job itself, but in the private world. Teachers have little stake in the communities in which they work; that is why it may be necessary to link more closely teachers' jobs and children's achievement. It is my guess that all children (except those with proven defects) would achieve if teachers' jobs depended on this. All would read and be at grade level—for teachers' sake.

It should also be noted, I think, that parents of children in Harlem cannot be expected to submit forever to the inferior education their children have been accorded. The rising militancy among minority groups has resulted from wariness and weariness with slum school procedures. This makes it even more difficult for those teachers who have traditionally been lax and inactive in working with parents toward resolving the problems children face in schools. They have helped to build no formal organizational structures toward doing this. Teachers feel a sense of danger and stress when these emergent social forms seem imminent. The move to greater decentralization of schools brings fear to teachers; it represents for them a reversal of previously approved interaction patterns. It is now they who will be responding to the suggestions and initiatives of parents, and not the reverse.

WHERE DO WE GO FROM HERE?

The teacher is not as trapped in Harlem School as is the child. He can go elsewhere; the poverty child cannot. The mode of recruitment into the social system of the slum school is different for teachers and children, as is the means of retention. The children's presence is not voluntary. And it ought not be surprising that parents will increasingly direct their efforts at neighborhood control of schools. School persons will object and will marshal efforts to prevent this; many teachers will flee to the suburbs. This will in many ways be the final irony, for it is the teachers who have asserted the alleged indifference of parents in the education of the children. The surge of community involvement will inevitably reveal teachers' own apathy and lack of concern. The myths about their own existence will return to haunt teachers. Indeed, the evidence is in many ways already accumulating.

There is no question that a more total approach must be taken to stem the tide of failure in the slum school. Government, university, public school, welfare agency, and neighborhood group have to come together. Failure to do this will only drive them further apart. The investment is in the future generations of our culture. The beginnings of societal change through the schools' efforts are to me a more relevant alternative than leaving initiative for needed change in the hands of the military, the church, business, or the various other institutional arrangements that too readily represent the corporate depersonalization of our lives. We have too long believed that we can neglect a large chunk of our population—the poor and the excluded—because our technological systems seem to maintain our material interests without the people we have neglected. In the long run, however, the major resource of any society is its people. And the essential essence of man as a culture-bearer is that he is capable of the will and the ingenuity to find a place for every person so that he can function with integrity and group support. This need will never be outlived by man as we now know him. I make no assertion in behalf of panhuman values in what I say here. There are perhaps too many exceptions in human cultures for any such assumptions. But insofar as all cultures are really systems of human reciprocity, it is not farfetched to suggest that we all have the capacity for assuming the credo: if you can do something for another person, you ought to do it. Harlem School would be quite a different place if this were the philosophy within which it operated. The teacher too has a chance at more meaningful personal realization. But the effort he makes will have to be much different from what it has been up to now.

Token heart,
Token soul,
Makes token love,
Has a token goal.

Inside, hollow;
Outside, slick;
Wants to thunder,
Can only click.

Fearful of trouble,
Hurries to calm.
Goes in like Du Bois,
Comes out like Tom.

Oh, token man, token man,
For you we grieve.
Oh, token man, token man,
What do you believe?

Heart's where it should be,
Inside his chest.
It's just disconnected
From the rest.

Climbing a ladder
With only one rung;
Like a fist in a hive
Without getting stung.

Token good.
Token bad,
Never happy,
Never sad.

Oh, token man, token man,
It makes no sense—
Oh, token man, token man—
Neutral existence.

One step taken
Is not a trip.
Single finger
Cannot grip.

Slivers of freedom,
Specks of truth,
Smidgens of justice,
"Progress", forsooth.

Taken so long,
Just to prepare.
Token that long
Has gotten you where?

Oh, token man, token man,
Hear my appeal:
Oh, token man, token man,
Make yourself real.

       (Weinberg 1966:22)

References

ALLPORT, GORDON W., 1961, "Values and Our Youth," *Teachers College Record* 63 (December):211–219.

ALSOP, JOSEPH, 1964, "The Real School Problem," *The New York Times* (March 18), p. 26.

APTHEKER, HERBERT, 1951, *A Documentary History of the Negro People in the United States*. New York: The Citadel Press.

ARENSBERG, CONRAD M., and ARTHUR H. NIEHOFF, 1964, *Introducing Social Change*. Chicago: Aldine Publishing Co.

————, and SOLON T. KIMBALL, 1965, *Culture and Community*. New York: Harcourt Brace Jovanovich, Inc.

ASHTON-WARNER, SYLVIA, 1963, *Teacher*. New York: Simon and Schuster, Inc.

AUSTIN, ERNEST H., JR., 1965, "I. Cultural Deprivation—A Few Questions," *Phi Delta Kappan* 47 (October):67–70.

BALDWIN, JAMES, 1963a, *The Fire Next Time*. New York: The Dial Press, Inc.

————, 1963b, *Nobody Knows My Name*. New York: Dell Publishing Company, Inc.

————, 1967, "Tell Me How Long the Train's Been Gone," *McCall's* 94 (February):118 ff.

BECKER, HOWARD S., 1960, "Notes on the Concept of Commitment," *The American Journal of Sociology* 66 (July):32–40.

BENEDICT, RUTH, 1959a, *Patterns of Culture*. Boston: Houghton Mifflin Company.

————, 1959b, *Race: Science and Politics*. New York: The Viking Press, Inc.

BERREMAN, GERALD D., 1968, "Is Anthropology Alive?," in *Reading in Anthropology, II*, Morton H. Fried, ed., New York: Thomas Y. Crowell Company, pp. 845–857.

BOAS, FRANZ, 1965, *The Mind of Primitive Man*. New York: The Free Press.

BOHANNAN, LAURA, 1966, "Shakespeare in the Bush," *Natural History* 75 (August-September):28–33.

BOHANNAN, PAUL J., 1968, "Field Anthropologists and Classroom Teachers," *Social Education* 32 (February):161–166.

BOWEN, ELENORE SMITH (pseud. of LAURA BOHANNAN), 1964, *Return to Laughter*. Garden City, N.Y.: The Natural History Library.

BROWN, CLAUDE, 1966, *Manchild in the Promised Land*. New York: The Macmillan Company.

BROWN, J. A. C., 1954, *The Social Psychology of Industry*. Baltimore: Penguin Books, Inc.

BROWN, STERLING A., 1962, "Strong Men," in *The Negro Today*, Herbert Aptheker, ed., New York: Marzani & Munsell, Inc., p. 14.

BRUNER, JEROME S., 1963, "Needed: A Theory of Instruction," *Educational Leadership* 20 (May):523–532.

————, 1960, *The Process of Education*. Cambridge: Harvard University Press.

————, 1966, "The Will To Learn," *Commentary* 41 (February), 41–46.

BURLEY, DAN, 1966, "The Dirty Dozen," in *The Book of Negro Humor,* Langston Hughes, ed., New York: Dodd, Mead & Company, Inc., pp. 119–121.

CAPLOVITZ, DAVID, 1963, *The Poor Pay More.* New York: The Free Press.

CLARK, BURTON R., 1962, *Educating the Expert Society.* San Francisco: Chandler Publishing Company.

CLARK, KENNETH B., 1965, *Dark Ghetto.* New York: Harper & Row, Publishers.

COLES, ROBERT, 1964, *Children of Crisis.* Boston: Little, Brown & Company.

————, 1965, "The Poor Don't Want To Be Middle Class," *The New York Times Magazine* (December 19):54–56, 58.

COLLIER, JOHN, 1947, *Indians of the Americas.* New York: New American Library.

CULLEN, COUNTEE, 1947, *On These I Stand.* New York: Harper & Row, Publishers.

DECTER, MIDGE, 1964, "The Negro and the New York Schools," *Commentary* 38 (September):25–34.

DEUTSCH, MARTIN, 1960, *Minority Group and Class Status as Related to Social and Personality Factors in Scholastic Achievement,* Monograph No. 2, Society for Applied Anthropology.

————, 1962, "Social and Psychological Perspective for the Facilitation of the Development of the Pre-school Child," reprinted from the Arden House Conference on Pre-School Enrichment of Socially Disadvantaged Children (December 16–18), pp. 1–32.

DEVEREUX, GEORGE, 1961, "The Idealized Self Image as an Obstacle in Inter-racial and Inter-sexual Diagnosis," *Abstracts,* publication of the American Anthropological Association on Its 60th Annual Meeting, Philadelphia (November), p. 7.

DIAMOND, STANLEY, 1964, "A Revolutionary Discipline," *Current Anthropology* 5 (December):432–436.

EDDY, ELIZABETH M., 1967, *Walk the White Line.* New York: Doubleday & Company, Inc.

FANTINI, MARIO D., and GERALD WEINSTEIN, 1967, "Taking Advantage of the Disadvantaged," *Teachers College Record* 69 (November):103–114.

FOSTER, GEORGE M., 1960–61, "Interpersonal Relations in Peasant Society." *Human Organization* 19 (Winter):174–178.

FUCHS, ESTELLE S., 1965, *School Boycott.* New York: Hunter College, Project TRUE.

GEERTZ, CLIFFORD, 1966, "The Impact of the Concept of Culture on the Concept of Man," *Bulletin of the Atomic Scientists* 22 (April):2–8.

GLADWIN, THOMAS, 1967, *Poverty U.S.A.* Boston: Little, Brown & Company.

GOLDBERG, ARTHUR J., 1964, "Are the Poor Less Equal?," *Current* (June-July): 57–60.

GOODENOUGH, WARD HUNT, 1963, *Cooperation in Change.* New York: Russell Sage Foundation.

GREENE, MARY FRANCES, and ORLETTA RYAN, 1965, *The Schoolchildren.* New York: Pantheon Books, Inc.

HALL, EDWARD T., 1959, *The Silent Language.* Greenwich, Conn.: Fawcett Publications, Inc.

————, 1964, "Adumbration as a Feature of Intercultural Communication," in *The Ethnography of Communication,* John J. Gumperz and Dell Hymes, eds., special publication of *American Anthropologist* 66 (December):154–163.

————, and WILLIAM FOOTE WHYTE, 1960, "Inter-cultural Communication: A Guide to Men of Action," *Human Organization* 19 (Spring):5–12.

HARRINGTON, MICHAEL, 1963, *The Other America.* New York: The Macmillan Company.

HART, C. W. M., 1954, "The Sons of Turimpi," *American Anthropologist* 56 (April): 242–261.

HAVIGHURST, ROBERT J., and BERNICE L. NEUGARTEN, 1957, *Society and Education.* Boston. Allyn and Bacon, Inc.

118 • REFERENCES

HECHINGER, FRED M., 1967, "The Teacher Gets What He Expects," *The New York Times* (August 13), p. E9.

HENRY, JULES, 1960, "A Cross-Cultural Outline of Education," *Current Anthropology* 1 (July):267–305.

————, 1963a, *Culture Against Man*. New York: Random House, Inc.

————, 1963b, "Reading for What?," *Teachers College Record* 65 (October): 35–46.

————, 1965, "White People's Time, Colored People's Time," *Trans-Action* 2 (March–April):31–34.

————, 1966, "Vulnerability in Education," *Teachers College Record* 68 (November):135–145.

HENTOFF, NAT, 1966, *Our Children Are Dying*. New York: The Viking Press, Inc.

HOLT, JOHN, 1965, *How Children Fail*. New York: Pitman Publishing Corporation.

HOMANS, GEORGE C., 1950, *The Human Group*. New York: Harcourt Brace Jovanovich, Inc.

HONIGMANN, JOHN J., 1963, *Understanding Culture*. New York: Harper & Row, Publishers.

HORWITZ, JULIUS, 1963, "The Grim State of Welfare," *Look* (April 2), pp. 72, 77–78, 80.

HOWE II, HAROLD, 1966, "Education's Most Crucial Issue," *Integrated Education* 4 (June–July):23–29.

HUGHES, LANGSTON, 1963, "Lenox Avenue Mural," in *American Negro Poetry*, Arna Bontemps, ed., New York: Hill and Wang, pp. 67–68.

JENCKS, CHRISTOPHER, 1966, "Who Should Control Education?," *Dissent* 13 (March–April):145–163.

JOHNSON, JAMES WELDON, n.d., mimeographed reprint of poem, no title given.

KHLEIF, BUD B., 1966, "A Socio-Cultural Framework for Studying Guidance in Public Schools," in *Guidance in American Education III*, Edward Landy and Arthur M. Kroll, eds., Cambridge: Harvard University Press, pp. 173–196.

KIMBALL, SOLON T., 1955a, "Anthropology and Communication," *Teachers College Record* 57 (November):64–71.

————, 1955b, "Problems of Studying American Culture," *American Anthropologist* 57 (December):1131–1142.

————, 1963, "Cultural Influences Shaping the Role of the Child," in *Education and Culture*, George D. Spindler, ed., New York: Holt, Rinehart and Winston, Inc., pp. 268–283.

————, 1965, "The Transmission of Culture," *Educational Horizons* 43 (Summer):161–186.

————, and JAMES McCLELLAN, 1962, *Education and the New America*. New York: Random House, Inc.

————, and MARION PEARSALL, 1954, *The Talladega Story*, University, Alabama: University of Alabama Press.

————, and MARION PEARSALL, 1965, "Event Analysis as an Approach to Community Study," in Conrad M. Arensberg and Solon T. Kimball, *Culture and Community*, New York: Harcourt Brace Jovanovich, Inc., pp. 281–289.

KLINEBERG, OTTO, 1958, *Race and Psychology*. Paris: UNESCO.

KOHL, HERBERT R., 1967a, *Teaching the Unteachable*. New York: A New York Review Book.

————, 1967b, *36 Children*. New York: New American Library.

KOZOL, JONATHAN, 1967, *Death at an Early Age*. Boston: Houghton Mifflin Company.

KROEBER, ALFRED L., 1966, *An Anthropologist Looks at History*. Berkeley: University of California Press.

LANDES, RUTH, 1965, *Culture in American Education*. New York: John Wiley & Sons, Inc.

LEAKS, SYLVESTER, 1963, "Talking about Harlem," *Freedomways* 3 (Summer): 263–265.

LESSER, ALEXANDER, 1961, "Education and the Future of Tribalism in the United States: The Case of the American Indian," *The Social Service Review* 35 (June): 1–9.

LEVI-STRAUSS, CLAUDE, 1961, *A World on the Wane,* John Russell, trans. New York: Criterion Books, Inc.

LEWIS, OSCAR, 1965, *La Vida.* New York: Random House, Inc.

————, 1966a, "The Culture of Poverty," *Scientific American* 215 (October): 19–25.

————, 1966b, "Even the Saints Cry," *Trans-Action* 4 (November): 18–23.

"Liberalism and the Negro: A Round-Table Discussion," 1964, *Commentary* 37 (March): 25–42.

LIEBOW, ELLIOT, 1967, *Tally's Corner: A Study of Negro Streetcorner Men.* Boston: Little, Brown & Company.

LINTON, RALPH, 1936, *The Study of Man.* New York: Appleton-Century-Crofts.

LITTLE, ROGER W., 1956, "The 'Sick Soldier' and the Medical Ward Officer," *Human Organization* 15 (Spring):22–24.

LOWELL, JAMES RUSSELL, 1956, "Stanzas on Freedom." In *A Pictorial History of the Negro in America,* Langston Hughes and Milton Meltzer, eds., New York: Crown Publishers, Inc., p. 105.

LYND, ROBERT S., 1964, *Knowledge for What?* New York: Grove Press, Inc.

MACKLER, BERNARD, and MORSLEY G. GIDDINGS, 1965, "Cultural Deprivation: A Study in Mythology," *Teachers College Record* 66 (April): 608–613.

MAYER, MARTIN, 1965, "Close to Midnight for the New York Schools," *The New York Times Magazine* (May 2), pp. 34–35, 104, 106–107.

MEAD, MARGARET, 1964, *Anthropology: A Human Science.* New York: D. Van Nostrand Company, Inc.

————, and MARTHA WOLFENSTEIN, eds., 1965, *Childhood in Contemporary Cultures.* Chicago: University of Chicago Press.

MILLENDER, DHARATHULA M., 1966, "Selecting Our Children's Books: Time for Some Changes," *Changing Education* 1 (Fall):8–13.

MINER, HORACE, 1956, "Body Ritual among the Nacirema," *American Anthropologist* 58 (June):503–507.

MITCHELL, MORRIS R., 1967, *World Education: Revolutionary Concept.* New York: Pageant Press, Inc.

MONTAGU, ASHLEY, 1964, *The Science of Man.* New York: The Odyssey Press, Inc.

————, 1966, "To Think and To Feel," in *Introduction to Education: A Comparative Analysis,* Donald K. Adams, ed., Belmont, California: Wadsworth Publishing Company, Inc., pp. 13–14.

MOORE, G. ALEXANDER, JR., 1964, *Urban School Days.* New York: Hunter College, Project TRUE.

MOYNIHAN, DANIEL P., 1967, "The President and the Negro: The Moment Lost," *A Commentary Report,* pp. 3–17.

MURDOCK, GEORGE PETER, 1945, "The Common Denominator of Cultures," in *The Science of Man in the World Crisis,* Ralph Linton, ed., New York: Columbia University Press, pp. 123–142.

"My Childhood," n.d., New York: Metromedia Films.

New York City Board of Education, 1929, *The Teacher's Handbook,* fifth edition (January 2).

New York Times, The, 1964, "Poverty No. 3 Cause of Death Here" (October 10), p. 59.

NIEHOFF, ARTHUR, ed., 1966, *A Casebook of Social Changes.* Chicago: Aldine Publishing Company.

ORNSTEIN, ALLAN C., 1967, "What It Is Really Like for Most Slum-School Teachers,"

Integrated Education 5 (October-November):48–52.

PADILLA, ELENA, 1958, *Up from Puerto Rico.* New York: Columbia University Press.

RIESSMAN, FRANK, 1962, *The Culturally Deprived Child.* New York: Harper & Row, Publishers.

————, 1964, "The Process of Learning," *Current* (June-July): 50–54.

————, and JOHN DAWKINS, eds., 1967, *Play it Cool in English.* Chicago: Follett Publishing Co.

SCHICKEL, RICHARD, 1964, "P.S. 165," *A Commentary Report,* pp. 3–11.

SEELEY, JOHN R., 1967, *The Americanization of the Unconscious.* New York: International Science Press.

SEXTON, PATRICIA CAYO, 1965, *Spanish Harlem.* New York: Harper & Row, Publishers.

STROM, ROBERT D., 1965, *Teaching in the Slum School.* Columbus, Ohio: Charles E. Merrill Books, Inc.

TAX, SOL, 1965, "Group Identity and Educating the Disadvantaged," in *Language Programs for the Disadvantaged,* publication of the National Council of Teachers of English, pp. 204–215.

THOMAS, PIRI, 1967, *Down These Mean Streets.* New York: Alfred A. Knopf.

THOMPSON, LAURA, 1965, "Is Applied Anthropology Helping to Develop a Science of Man?," *Human Organization* 24 (Winter):277–287.

TORRANCE, E. PAUL, 1962, *Guiding Creative Talent.* Englewood Cliffs, N.J.: Prentice-Hall, Inc.

————, 1963, "The Creative Personality and the Ideal Pupil," *Teachers College Record* 65 (December):220–226.

TROW, MARTIN, 1957, "Comment on 'Participant Observation and Interviewing: A Comparison,'" *Human Organization* 16 (Fall):33–35.

TURNBULL, COLIN M., 1966, "A People Apart," *Natural History* 75 (October):8–14.

————, 1963, *The Lonely African.* New York: Doubleday & Company, Inc.

VAN GENNEP, ARNOLD, 1960, *The Rites of Passage,* Monika B. Vizedom and Gabriella L. Caffee, trans., Chicago: University of Chicago Press.

WAX, MURRAY, 1963, "American Indian Education as a Cultural Transaction," *Teachers College Record* 64 (May):693–704.

————, *et al.,* 1964, *Formal Education in an American Indian Community,* Supplement, *Social Problems* 2 (Spring).

WEINBERG, MEYER, 1966, "Token Man," *Integrated Education* 4 (June-July):22.

WOLCOTT, HARRY F., 1967, *A Kwakiutl Village and School.* New York: Holt, Rinehart and Winston, Inc.

WRIGHT, NATHAN, JR., 1967, *Black Power and Urban Unrest.* New York: Hawthorn Books, Inc.

ZAMOFF, RICHARD, 1966, "The Attitudinally Disadvantaged Teacher," *The Urban Review* 1 (December):875–876.